Bridging the Gap

Trade Laws in the Canadian-U.S. Negotiations

Murray G. Smith
with
C. Michael Aho
and
Gary N. Horlick

Canadian-American Committee
Sponsored by
■ C.D. Howe Institute (Canada)
■ National Planning Association (U.S.A.)

Contents

11-19-04um

Foreword

Canada and the United States have embarked on a historic set of negotiations aimed at strengthening the world's largest bilateral economic relationship. In *Canadian-U.S. Trade Options*, the Canadian-American Committee's September 1985 statement, the Committee identified the economic benefits to both countries of achieving more open and stable trade and investment relations.

Both countries share some common objectives in the trade talks but each brings quite different priorities to the negotiating table. Canada seeks the elimination of tariffs and nontariff barriers, greater security of access to the U.S. market, and better mechanisms for resolution of trade disputes. The United States seeks the elimination of higher Canadian tariffs, a more open and stable environment for investment and services trade, and better protection of intellectual property. Although both sides seek to reduce provincial and state barriers to trade in goods and services, the United States attaches a higher priority to eliminating provincial nontariff trade barriers.

In light of these different priorities, as well as divergent domestic interests, a mutually acceptable agreement is proving difficult to achieve. Subsidies and countervailing duties, as well as antidumping and other import relief laws, have emerged as thorny areas for negotiation. This study explores options for bridging the gap on this key negotiating issue. Reconciling Canadian and U.S. perspectives on this issue is likely to be critical to the success of the negotiations.

The stakes are high. Bilateral trade in goods totals U.S.$125 billion — more than between any two other countries in the world. Each country is the other's largest trading partner. The United States purchases almost four-fifths of Canadian merchandise exports while Canada accounts for one-quarter of U.S. exports.

In recent years, considerable attention has focused on the bilateral payments balance. Americans are concerned about Canada's surplus in merchandise trade, which reached U.S.$17 billion in 1985, while Canadians are concerned about U.S. trade surpluses in secondary manufactures and services. Services trade — such as travel and tourism, advertising, engineering, entertainment, and finance — is not included in merchandise trade data. As a result, Canada's deficit on services transactions with the United States — amounting to U.S.\$2 billion — is often overlooked.

Investment is another important element in the bilateral account. Although Canadian direct investment in the United States is growing rapidly, holdings of U.S. firms in Canada are much larger in absolute terms, and are larger than in any other country. Also, Canadians have debt obligations of U.S.\$72 billion to U.S. residents. As a result of these investment links, the bilateral current account is approximately balanced by interest and dividend payments and the cumulation of retained earnings.

Failure to establish more effective rules for commercial relations between the two countries can create new bilateral frictions that may threaten the benefits both countries now enjoy. Moreover, as the Committee documented in *The Global Competitive Struggle: Challenges to the United States and Canada*, industries in both countries increasingly are subject to offshore competition. Expanded trading opportunities in the North American market will improve the international competitiveness of many of these industries.

The Committee publication *Weathering the Storm: Canadian-U.S. Relations, 1980–83* illustrates how differences in national perceptions can lead to unilateral actions by one of the partners. Such actions encourage confrontation and create the potential for a mutually damaging cycle of retaliation. The current bilateral trade negotiations offer an opportunity for the two countries to explore basic differences in their approaches to economic policy areas, such as subsidies and investment, that have been a source of bilateral tensions. Common rules and procedures could be developed that could help avoid disputes or aid their resolution.

The Canadian-American Committee is publishing this volume, the main part of which consists of a paper by Murray G. Smith, who serves as the Canadian Director of Research for the Committee, in an effort to contribute to the negotiating process. Smith's paper was discussed at the Committee's September 26, 1986, meeting in Ottawa, and commentaries on the paper were presented by C. Michael Aho, Senior Fellow-Economics, Council on Foreign Relations, Inc., New York, and Gary N. Horlick, Partner, O'Melveny & Myers,

Washington. Barry A. Norris prepared the manuscript for publication; he was assisted by Cordelia Sharpe. Publication by the Committee does not mean that all members specifically endorse the points or conclusions the authors make. The Committee believes, however, this analysis of the issues deserves consideration in both countries.

Stephen C. Eyre
Co-chairman

Adam H. Zimmerman
Co-chairman

Negotiating Trade Laws: Possible Approaches

Murray G. Smith

Introduction

The outcome of negotiations on the bilateral application of trade laws could prove critical to the overall success of the Canadian-U.S. trade negotiations. From the start, Canadians have stressed that a key objective in the negotiations is greater security of access to the U.S. market.[1] By lack of secure access, Canadians mean:

- the manner in which the United States' use of trade remedy laws can frustrate Canadian companies' access to the U.S. market;
- the ease with which imports from Canada are swept up in measures aimed at other countries; and
- the continual threat of unilateral changes by the United States in the rules of the game.[2]

Although U.S. exporters may experience similar difficulties with Canadian trade laws, congressional leaders and administration spokesmen have suggested that the United States is unwilling to alter, even on a reciprocal basis, its existing trade laws and procedures as they apply to imports from Canada.

The purpose of this paper is to explore some of the differences between Canadian and U.S. perceptions on the application of trade laws and to examine various approaches to the negotiations on this key issue that could help avoid a potential deadlock. If an impasse over the negotiation of trade laws occurred, it likely would jeopardize the entire bilateral trade negotiations.

Outline of the Study

The next section of this paper defines the problem that import relief laws pose for the bilateral trading relationship. The third section then turns to an examination of Canadian and U.S. perspec-

---

[1]See the Hon. J. Kelleher, Report by Minister for International Trade, September 17, 1985, and the Rt. Hon. Brian Mulroney, Statement to the House of Commons, September 26, 1985, in *Canadian Trade Negotiations* (Ottawa: Department of External Affairs, 1985).

[2]Kelleher, Report by Minister for International Trade, p. 68.

tives on the use of trade laws. The fourth section outlines the economic, political, and international factors that have influenced both countries' import relief laws. The fifth section explores how negotiations might resolve some of the underlying problems. It analyzes various negotiating approaches to the key bilateral problem areas on the basis of past experience with regional trading arrangements. The paper then turns to the strategic implications of potential linkages between the bilateral agreement and multilateral negotiations under the auspices of the General Agreement on Tariffs and Trade (GATT). The final sections assess the various negotiating approaches and examine the question of how to balance the two countries' complex interests on import relief laws as part of an overall bilateral agreement.

Defining the Problem

The existence and use of import relief laws — a system of laws and regulatory procedures that allows domestic industries to seek redress from what is regarded as unfair or disruptive import competition — is an increasingly contentious issue between the Canada and the United States. As tariffs have been lowered following successive rounds of multilateral negotiations, industries threatened by increased imports have tended to resort to import tribunals seeking antidumping and countervailing duties or emergency import quotas and surcharges.

The proliferation of these measures and the increased tendency to resort to them are not new phenomena. As long ago as 1963, the Canadian-American Committee noted a systematic relationship between congressional actions to grant the president authority to participate in trade negotiations and the elaboration of import relief laws:

> The power of the President to reduce U.S. tariffs continues to be derived from the Trade Agreements Act, which was further extended by Congress in 1948, 1949, 1951, 1953, 1954, 1955, and 1958. Since 1948, congressional renewals of the Trade Agreements Act have incorporated numerous safeguards to protect U.S. producing interests against intensified import competition.[3]

The trend toward elaboration of import relief laws accelerated with the *Trade Act of 1974*, which granted negotiating authority for the Tokyo Round of multilateral negotiations, and the *Trade Agreements*

---

[3]H.S. Piquet, *The U.S. Trade Expansion Act of 1962: How Will It Affect Canadian-American Trade?* (Washington, D.C.; Montreal: Canadian-American Committee, 1963), p. 4.

Act of 1979, which implemented the Tokyo Round agreements.[4] This trend could continue if tariffs were largely eliminated by a comprehensive trade agreement.

In both countries, import relief legislation is two-pronged. One prong consists of remedies intended to limit what are perceived as unfair foreign trade practices. Antidumping and countervailing duties fall into this category, as do other remedies against such practices as copyright or patent infringement and discriminatory regulatory policies. Both countries require that an independent tribunal make a determination that an industry is experiencing "material injury" — or the threat of such injury — before antidumping or countervailing duties are imposed.

The other prong, sometimes referred to as the "escape clause" or as "safeguards", is intended to provide temporary relief to domestic industries that are suffering from surges in imports. If industries can demonstrate "serious injury" from imports — a stricter definition and more difficult to prove than "material injury" — then quotas or additional tariffs may be imposed.

Bilateral negotiations on import relief laws are likely to be difficult because of differing perceptions of how the two countries' domestic institutions and policies operate. The terms "fair" and "unfair" trade, for example, are highly emotive and subjective, and it could be very difficult to agree on what constitutes fair trade. As John Jackson, a U.S. expert on international trade law, observes:

> What is often surprising, however, is that even nations with very similar economic systems, such as two industrial country market economies, can find that minor variations in their economic systems can create situations which have the appearance of unfairness. These situations may have arisen almost completely by accident. That is, there may have been no intention to engage in any practice which is deemed 'unfair'.[5]

Jackson then suggests a different term to describe the economic frictions that arise between countries:

> I have termed this problem the "interface" problem....When it is desired that two computers of different makes work together, it often takes some kind of "interface" mechanism or programme to mediate between them and to translate the language of one machine to that of the other. Likewise, when two societies with even minor

---

[4]R. de C. Grey, *Trade Policy in the 1980s: An Agenda for Canadian-U.S. Relations* (Montreal: C.D. Howe Institute, 1981).
[5]J.H. Jackson, "Achieving a Balance in International Trade," *International Business Lawyer* (April 1986), p. 124.

economic differences desire to work together, frictions or misunderstandings can occur unless there is an interface mechanism. To a certain extent, the national trade laws and the GATT Bretton Woods System are operating today as a rather crude interface mechanism. The problem often is that policy leaders have not perceived this, but instead believe that it is necessary to characterise some practices as "unfair" or "illegal". In at least some of the international trade problems which exist today, a more neutral terminology and policy approach that would avoid moral overtones may operate with greater utility for world economic welfare and harmony.[6]

This analysis focuses on the issues associated with Jackson's "interface" problem in the specific context of negotiating a comprehensive bilateral trade agreement that takes the form of a free trade area (FTA) under GATT rules. It may not be self-evident that Canada and the United States are negotiating an FTA, but the U.S. administration explicitly obtained fast-track negotiating authority to negotiate one with Canada. (The broader elements of a possible Canadian-American Free Trade Area [CAFTA] are spelled out elsewhere.[7]) The negotiation of import relief laws will occur as part of the overall negotiation of an FTA agreement. Although the structure and precise details of an FTA agreement remain conjectural, pending the outcome of the negotiations, some of the more likely elements regarding trade in goods can be summarized briefly:

- bilateral elimination of tariffs and quotas in the industrial sector;
- rules of origin to determine which products qualify for duty-free trade;
- transition arrangements governing the timing of tariff reductions; and
- rules governing such nontariff barriers as government procurement preferences for local suppliers.

It is much less certain what might be negotiable on the issues of investment and trade in services. The United States regards obtaining agreements on these issues as priority objectives, and Canada's willingness to negotiate on these matters will be influenced by the extent to which the United States is prepared to negotiate on the application of trade laws.

Developing mutually agreed rules for bilateral trade will require that differences in Canadian and U.S. perceptions be reconciled and

---

[6]Ibid.
[7]See R.G. Lipsey and M.G. Smith, *Taking the Initiative: Canada's Trade Options in a Turbulent World*, Observation no. 27 (Toronto: C.D. Howe Institute, 1985).

that both countries' interests be carefully balanced. Although the issues are complex and will test the ingenuity and skill of negotiators, the role of private decisionmakers in both countries in articulating their views and concerns to policymakers will be critical to the successful conclusion of the actual agreement.

Canadian and U.S. Perceptions

The task of reconciling Canadian and U.S. perspectives on trade laws — let alone resolving the issues — is in itself a very difficult challenge. The problem is illustrated by the semantic debate on how one should refer to the trade laws. One Canadian expert, Rodney Grey, has coined the term "contingent protection" to describe the U.S. system of trade laws and procedures.[8] U.S. officials and congressional leaders reject this term, instead describing U.S. trade laws as "trade remedy" laws. Behind the semantic debate lie sharply different perspectives over whether trade laws are protectionist or are measures intended to redress various types of inequities or imbalances in trade.

In an effort to avoid this semantic debate and the emotional appeals that lie behind it, this paper uses the term "trade laws", and focuses only on one important component of the arcane labyrinth of trade laws both countries have erected: import relief laws that currently apply to goods imported from the other country.

The Bilateral Dimension

From the U.S. perspective, existing U.S. import legislation provides a transparent, nonpolitical system for dealing with trade disputes that involve allegations of unfair trade and import disruptions caused by products acknowledged to be fairly traded. To Canadian exporters, however, the U.S. system seems to provide opportunities for import-competing interests to harass Canadian firms by subjecting them to the cost of defending expensive legal proceedings as well as to the risk of apparently arbitrary trade barriers being imposed on Canadian products. Canadians feel, moreover, that the recent decision by the U.S. International Trade Administration (ITA) to reverse its 1983 ruling on softwood lumber (which found Canadian stumpage policies — fees charged for the sale of timber — not to be countervailable subsidies under U.S. law) undermines the credibility of the claim that the U.S. system is nonpolitical.

Although the two countries have quite similar import regulation systems, asymmetries in trade and production between them mean

---

[8]Grey, *Trade Policy in the 1980s*, p. 15.

that Canada has a greater interest in restricting application of import relief legislation than does the United States. In the smaller Canadian economy, exports frequently account for a relatively larger share of production, and most of those exports go to the United States. Thus, the risk of U.S. import restrictions or duties significantly increases the risk to investment in new production facilities in Canada. The same cannot be said of the United States. Although plants located in U.S. border states may send a high proportion of their output to Canada, it is relatively easy for them to shift sales to other parts of the United States if Canada imposes import duties.

Canada's dependence on exports to the United States can create problems from a U.S. perspective as well. As a 1972 statement by the Canadian-American Committee observed presciently:

> [G]iven the high percentage of Canadian production exported to the United States, Canadian policies to head off unemployment through subsidizing production might often appear in American eyes to be export subsidies, and be answered as such.[9]

The potential application of U.S. countervailing duties is a particular source of concern to Canadians because the threat of such duties impinges on Canada's choice of domestic economic policies. This was first illustrated by the 1973 Michelin tire decision, in which the United States found Canadian regional development subsidies to be a countervailable subsidy. Prior to that decision, the U.S. Treasury had applied countervailing duties only to more specific cases of explicit export subsidies. Under present U.S. practice, countervailing duties can be imposed on any domestic subsidies that are not widely available, although recent decisions by the U.S. Court of International Trade cast some doubt on even this restriction.[10]

These court decisions, and a subsequent administrative review by the ITA, were factors in the 1986 decision by a U.S. producer group — the Coalition for Fair Lumber Imports — to resubmit a petition seeking countervailing duties on softwood lumber.

The Gibbons bill, introduced in 1985 and incorporated into the omnibus trade bill of 1986, represented a legislative effort to broaden further the definition of subsidy in U.S. countervailing duty law in a manner that was aimed at Canadian resource policies. This provision was intended to overturn the ITA's 1983 softwood products de-

---

[9]Canadian-American Committee, *The New Environment for Canadian-American Relations* (Washington, D.C.; Montreal: Canadian-American Committee, 1972), p. 34.
[10]See *Bethlehem Steel Corp v. United States and Highveld Steel and Vanadium Corp*, U.S. Court of International Trade (1984); and *Cabot Corp. v. United States*, U.S. Court of International Trade (1985).

cision. Further, congressional action was pre-empted by the U.S. Commerce Department's October 1986 preliminary ruling that Canadian stumpage policies constituted a subsidy. Canadians see this ruling as an encroachment on their economic and political sovereignty. In their view, an agency of the U.S. government is passing judgment on the long-standing resource tenure systems and stumpage practices of the Canadian provinces by declaring them to constitute unfair trade. Thus, the trend toward a broadening of the U.S. definition of what constitutes a countervailable subsidy operates as an increasing constraint on the domestic policies of Canadian governments.

Canada finds itself in a uniquely difficult position on subsidies and countervailing duties. More than any other country, Canada is vulnerable to the imposition of U.S. countervailing duties directed against foreign subsidies. The subsidy wars that have occurred between the European Community (EC) and the United States on agriculture provide a typical case where Canada has been caught in the crossfire, because there is no effective mechanism to control subsidies that increase exports to third-country markets.

To be fair, U.S. exporters often express concerns about Canada's import relief laws as well. Antidumping duties are the most frequently applied remedy in Canadian trade legislation. An indication of the relative frequency of antidumping actions in the two countries is evident from a comparison of Tables 1 and 2. During the 1980–85 period, there were ten U.S. antidumping actions on Canadian products, five of which were found to cause injury. During the same period, there were 31 Canadian antidumping actions on U.S. products, with injury being found in 27 cases.

Despite Canadian concerns about U.S. trade legislation, Canadian trade legislation has evolved along similar lines and now has broadly similar regulatory procedures. As a result of the 1984 *Special Import Measures Act*, for example, Canada now has countervailing duty laws and procedures analogous to those of the United States. Indeed, some of the similarities between Canadian and U.S. import relief systems are the result of the efforts of U.S. negotiators to achieve more transparent administration of, and procedures for, Canadian import relief laws. The negotiation of the Antidumping Code during the Kennedy Round of the 1960s meant that Canada had to abandon its "automatic" antidumping system administered by customs officials and introduce the requirement that a quasi-judicial tribunal make an injury finding before antidumping duties are imposed.[11] Very recently, Canada has moved

---

[11]R. de C. Grey, *The Development of the Canadian Antidumping System* (Montreal: Private Planning Association of Canada, 1973).

Table 1
U.S. Antidumping Investigations
of Canadian Exports, 1980–85

Year	Product	ITC & ITA finding	Action
1980	asphalt products	negative	—
	canned clams	negative	—
	sugars and syrups	affirmative	quotas
1983	potatoes	negative	—
	dried salted codfish	affirmative	duty of 20.75%
1984	choline chlorides	affirmative	duties imposed
	raspberries	affirmative	duty of .99%
	egg filler flats	negative	—
1985	rock salt	negative	—
	tubular steel products	affirmative	average duty of 19%

Sources: United States, International Trade Commission, *Annual Report*, various issues; and United States, Office of the U.S. Trade Representative, *Annual Report of the President on the Trade Agreements Program*, various issues.

to implement changes in customs valuation procedures negotiated during the Tokyo Round that reduced the discretion of Canadian customs officials to adjust the value of imported goods.

The negotiation of a bilateral agreement is an opportunity to focus on the pragmatic resolution of some of the problems that arise out of the high level of economic interdependence between the two countries. Maintaining existing import relief legislation and procedures could frustrate many of the potential benefits to both countries of removing tariff and nontariff barriers to trade. The existing systems provide considerable potential for harassment of trade between the two countries. In the more competitive North American market environment that would result from the removal of other trade barriers, greater incentives could be created for firms in one country to launch import relief actions against competitors that were producing in, or obtaining components from, the partner country. The risk of such actions could have a chilling effect on trade and could pose particular difficulties for multinational firms — Canadian as well as U.S. — seeking to rationalize their operations on both sides of the border.

Beyond the potential for abuse of existing laws, either country might act in future to redefine its import relief laws in ways that undermine the reductions in trade barriers agreed to in the original negotiations. If the negotiations do not deal with these issues, there is a risk that subsequent behavior contrary to the spirit, if not the letter, of the agreement could cause the agreement to unravel. Unless the two governments can deal with the underlying "interface"

Table 2
Canadian Antidumping Investigations
of U.S. Exports, 1980–85

Year	Product	Injury finding
1980	forklift trucks	affirmative
	pool and snooker tables	affirmative
	airless paint sprayers	negative
	methyl ethyl ketone peroxide	affirmative
	citric acid and sodium citrate	affirmative
	custom wheel rims	affirmative
	sporting ammunition	affirmative
1981	juvenile products	affirmative
	vehicle washing equipment	affirmative
	peroxides	affirmative[a]
	multilink intercom systems	affirmative
	chelating agents	negative
	radiator heaters	affirmative
	steel rules	affirmative
1982	peroxides	affirmative[a]
	bottoming agents	affirmative
1983	band saw blades	affirmative
	induction motors	affirmative
	toilet seats	negative
	soda ash	affirmative
1984	plate coils	affirmative
	contact lenses	affirmative
	stainless steel pipe	affirmative
	potatoes	affirmative
	refined sugar	affirmative
1985	porcelain insulators	affirmative
	abrasion-resistant steel pipe	affirmative
	plywood (concrete forming panels)	negative
	photo albums	affirmative
	rail car axles	affirmative

[a] The Antidumping Tribunal's initial ruling was reversed by the Federal Court, which ordered a rehearing of the case.

Source: Canadian Import Tribunal, *Annual Report*, various issues.

problems between their highly interdependent economies, retaining the existing crude interface of national import relief laws and procedures could create greater problems for bilateral economic relations in the future.

In a more positive vein, the elimination of trade barriers would alter significantly the rationale for some existing import relief laws. Although there may be immediate domestic pressures to broaden the application of these laws as tariffs are reduced, the removal of tariffs and other nontariff barriers to trade — such as government procurement preferences — would reduce greatly the scope for predatory activity. Firms that operate in cartelized and protected home markets are better able to sustain competitive practices that are damaging to foreign rivals. Open borders, however, limit the ability of firms to engage in such strategies and also can constrain subsidy policies. As Banks and Tumlir observe:

> Analysis of the 'impediments' to adjustment and growth reveals the key role of border protection. Without protection against imports, neither cartels (in product and labour markets) nor subsidies would pose such a problem. (If steel could be imported into the European Community without quantitative limitations, subsidy needs would soon exceed the capacity of national budgets.)[12]

Furthermore, with open borders, competitive conditions in particular industries will become more closely aligned over time, reducing the potential for import disruption from bilateral trade.

Factors Influencing the Evolution of Trade Laws

This section outlines some of the economic, political, international, and historical factors that have interacted to create the extraordinarily complex systems of import relief laws in Canada and the United States. The discussion focuses on the common elements operating in the two countries.

Economic Rationales

Economic rationales may not be the dominant factors influencing the design of import relief laws, but proponents of such laws frequently cite them in support of their position. Because of these economic arguments, policymakers are persuaded to regard as invalid the normal presumption that international trade benefits both exporting and importing countries. Let us examine these arguments.

Dumped or subsidized goods can have predatory effects. This rationale has a long history, having been cited when Canada introduced antidumping legislation in 1904. At that time, the Canadian Minister of Finance stated that:

> the trust or combine, having obtained command and control of its own market and finding that it will have a surplus of goods, sets out to obtain command of a neighbouring market, and for the purpose of obtaining control...will put aside all reasonable considerations with regard to the cost or fair price of the goods....If these trusts and combines in the high tariff countries would come un-

---

[12]G. Banks and J. Tumlir, "The Political Problem of Adjustment," *The World Economy* 9 (1986): 149.

der obligations...to supply us with these goods at the lowest prices for the next fifty years, it would probably be the part of wisdom for us to close up some of our industries and turn the energies of our people to other branches. But surely none of us imagine that when their high tariff trusts and combines send goods into Canada at sacrifice prices they do it for any benevolent purpose. They are not worrying about the good of the people of Canada. They send the goods here with the hope and the expectation that they will crush out the native Canadian industries.[13]

The introduction of antidumping legislation in the United States also was based on the rationale of predatory effects. Indeed, the *Antidumping Act of 1916* provided that dumping was unlawful if "done with the intent" of destroying U.S. industries or monopolizing U.S. trade.[14] Although the 1916 act still applies, it has been superseded by the *Antidumping Act of 1921* and the *Trade Agreements Act of 1979*, which require a less stringent "injury" test before antidumping duties are levied.

While antidumping duties have been used to prevent predation by private firms, the use of countervailing duties has been justified on the grounds that foreign subsidies can damage domestic industries and create a potential monopoly for foreign suppliers of particular products.[15] This argument has particular relevance to targeted subsidies intended to aid the development of new technology and products.

Subsidies distort international trade and reduce world economic welfare. The argument behind this rationale for import relief laws is that even if the imposition of countervailing duties is contrary to the economic interests of the importing country, the existence of procedures to investigate foreign subsidies and to impose countervailing duties when necessary contributes to better functioning of the world economy.[16]

Although it is widely accepted in the international community that subsidies distort trade, there has been considerable disagreement about the extent to which different types of subsidies actually have this effect. For much of the postwar period, efforts of countries within the GATT and the Organisation for Economic Cooperation and Development (OECD) to limit the use of subsidies as

---

[13]The 1904 Budget Speech of the Canadian Minister of Finance, W.S. Fielding, cited in R. de C. Grey, "Trade Policy and the System of Contingency Protection in the Perspective of Competition Policy" (Paper prepared for the Department of External Affairs, released under the *Freedom of Information Act*, Ottawa, May 1986), pp. 11–12.
[14]Ibid., p. 12.
[15]G.C. Hufbauer and J.S. Erb, *Subsidies in International Trade* (Washington, D.C.: Institute for International Economics, 1984), p. 21; and Jackson, "Achieving a Balance," p. 125.
[16]Ibid.

well as actions under national countervailing duty laws were directed against export subsidies — subsidies explicitly linked to increased export sales. During the 1970s, however, concerns were raised about domestic subsidies that may indirectly influence export performance to varying degrees. It has been much more difficult to reach an international consensus on these latter issues.

Injurious imports impose adjustment costs on firms and workers. Another economic rationale for import relief measures is that sudden surges in imports result in unemployment and in underutilization of plant and equipment, and that these effects would be reduced significantly if more orderly shifts in trade occurred. Indeed, some argue that adjustment costs should be the sole concern of trade policy. As Richard Cooper states:

> [P]erhaps we should not worry so much about government subsidies to economic activity — or rather government intervention of all types — as far as their effects on foreign trade are concerned, provided the interventions are introduced sufficiently gradually so that they do not impose acute adjustment costs on economic activities outside the country in question.[17]

Economic Critiques

As the quote from Cooper suggests, there are economic critiques of, as well as economic rationales for, import relief laws. These critiques can be summarized briefly.

Import relief laws can inhibit adjustment by domestic industries to international competition. Temporary protection may be warranted to reduce adjustment costs borne by workers and firms, but if the measures are badly timed, the effect may be to increase adjustment costs. Also, firms may not restructure production and upgrade product lines when import relief is granted.

Countervailing and antidumping duties can prevent trade that is of benefit to the importing country. Consumer benefits and efficiency gains from trade that accrue to the economy are not taken into account when countervailing and antidumping duties are imposed.[18] Taken to extremes, imposing duties on all trade regarded as "unfair" harkens back to the doctrine of the scientific tariff, which would prevent any of the gains from trade among countries being realized.

---

[17]R.N. Cooper, "U.S. Policies and Practices on Subsidies in International Trade," in Steven J. Warnecke, ed., *International Trade and Industrial Policies* (New York: Holmes & Meier, 1978), p. 120.
[18]See K. Stegemann, "Anti-dumping Policy and the Consumer," *Journal of World Trade Law* 19 (1985): 466–484.

Political Pressures

In addition to economic arguments for and against import relief laws, domestic political pressures also play an important role in shaping the import relief systems of Canada and the United States.

Maintaining a political coalition to support open markets requires taking action against unfair competition. In the United States, with its more open lobbying process, it is evident that the efforts of successive administrations to obtain congressional authorization to negotiate tariff reductions have been aided by legislative actions and administrative changes that have broadened the application of U.S. import relief measures.[19] In Canada, a similar process seems to operate, because Canada also has broadened the application of its import relief laws.

Displaced workers and firms with declining sales resist import competition. Imports can play a highly visible role in reducing domestic firms' sales, resulting in underutilization of plant capacity and dislocation of workers. It is not surprising, therefore, that import-competing interests seek the imposition of trade barriers.

Permitting "due process" for domestic interests deflects domestic and international pressures on policymakers. Legislators often find that the existence of a mandatory import relief system can help deflect pressures from their constituents for overt protectionist measures that restrict imports.[20] At the same time, nondiscretionary import relief laws help deflect pressures from foreign governments when such measures are imposed.

International and Historical Factors

A number of international and historical factors have shaped import relief systems. International arrangements act to constrain and shape domestic pressures for import relief measures. At the same time, national governments revise international agreements in response to domestic lobbying pressures.

The GATT has sanctioned remedies against unfair trade and import disruption. Since the GATT has permitted countries to impose import duties on dumped or subsidized goods and temporary im-

---

[19]I.M. Destler, *Making Foreign Economic Policy* (Washington, D.C.: Brookings Institution, 1980), pp. 129–167.
[20]Ibid.

port restraints in industries experiencing disruptive surges in imports, these measures have become the focus of efforts to limit import competition.

Subsidies can be used to offset negotiated reductions in trade barriers; thus, actions against unfair trade preserve the sanctity of trade agreements. According to this argument, trade agreements such as the GATT or an FTA are international contracts consisting of negotiated reductions in tariff and nontariff barriers to trade. Since subsidies can be used to counteract improvements in market access that foreign producers obtain as a result of trade negotiations, disciplines on subsidies can help to preserve the sanctity of the contract.

International codification of import procedures and remedies has encouraged industrial countries to adopt similar import regimes. Rodney Grey has argued eloquently that the process of negotiating international agreements on import relief laws can lead to the proliferation of protective mechanisms that are contrary to the stated objective of liberalizing trade.[21] This proliferation occurs because each country seeks to ensure that its domestic import regulatory procedures are codified in international agreements. Subsequently, import-competing interests in each country lobby their domestic authorities to incorporate the import relief laws and procedures of other countries, which the international agreements permit. For example, Canada's *Special Import Measures Act*, passed in 1984, embodies features of U.S. and European Community import relief laws as well as procedures permitted by Tokyo Round codes that were previously unavailable to domestic firms seeking relief from import competition.

International negotiations involve compromise between different perspectives on particular issues. Subsidies and countervailing duties were a key issue in the Tokyo Round, yet the gap between the negotiating positions of the United States and the EC impeded the development of an effective Subsidies Code. The United States sought to discipline other countries' subsidies, while other countries sought to limit the application of U.S. countervailing duties through the introduction of an injury test into U.S. countervailing duty procedures. A compromise was achieved whereby the United States introduced the injury test for countries signing the Subsidies Code

---

[21]See Grey, *Trade Policy in 1980s*.

and broadened the definition of countervailable subsidies. But countervailing duties are imposed only on imports entering a country's domestic market; they are not effective remedies against foreign subsidies that displace exports. Although the Subsidies Code attempts to deal with this issue, it has proven ineffective, as has been demonstrated through the recent escalation of the global rivalry in export subsidies for agricultural products.

Negotiating Approaches

As part of the comprehensive negotiations on a Canadian-U.S. trade agreement, a number of approaches to the more specific negotiations on import relief laws have been suggested. These include:

• Granting national treatment to goods and services originating in the other country. National treatment means that foreign producers receive the same treatment under legislation and public policies as is afforded domestic producers. In practical terms, this amounts to the two countries' being exempted from the application of each other's import relief laws.
• Negotiating revised criteria for bilateral import relief measures.
• Maintaining bilateral import relief laws, but administering them jointly with the objective of limiting their bilateral application.
• Retaining separate national import relief systems, but introducing procedural changes in each country's domestic process and new standards of injury determination.

This section examines the main concerns that import relief laws address — dumping by private firms, government subsidies, and disruptive import competition — and examines how the various negotiating approaches could be used to resolve some of the central negotiating issues.

Dumping

The most contentious private business practice that import relief laws govern is dumping. In its strictest sense, dumping involves selling goods in the export market at a price that is lower than that at which the same goods are sold in the domestic market. In the domestic market, this is referred to as price discrimination, which is often linked to predatory pricing behavior. The legal definition of dumping also refers to import prices that are below the full cost of production, regardless of whether dumping — in the sense of price discrimination — actually occurs.

National Treatment

Various negotiating approaches to antidumping duties are possible, but it is the national treatment, or bilateral exemption, option that makes the most logical sense. Removing tariff barriers (which segment national markets) would remove the potential for predatory dumping based on a protected home market. Furthermore, eliminating antidumping procedures also would remove some of the potential for harassment of trade between the two countries.

Exempting bilateral trade completely from antidumping duties and procedures is feasible, at least in principle, because each country has domestic laws directed against unfair pricing. The exemption would involve each country affording national treatment in the application of price discrimination laws.[22] Here is how this would work. If a company in Cleveland sells a product in its local market at a higher price than it sells that product in Hamilton, then the company would be subject to Canadian price discrimination laws. If the same company sells a product at a lower price in the Buffalo market, then it would be subject to U.S. price discrimination laws. If antidumping duties were eliminated, domestic price discrimination laws, such as Robinson-Patman in the United States and Section 34 of the *Competition Act* in Canada, still would apply and would provide remedies against pricing practices that could seriously damage competition.

Economists and U.S. jurists have criticized price discrimination laws in recent years because these laws can limit price competition that is not predatory and that is beneficial to society.[23] Canada has seldom used price discrimination laws. In the United States, recent trends in antitrust policy and enforcement have permitted firms greater flexibility in pricing strategies and have reduced the likelihood that price discounts will be sanctioned under price discrimination laws.

In both countries, trends in the enforcement of antidumping laws on the one hand and domestic price discrimination laws on the other have tended to diverge in recent years. Price discrimination laws increasingly have recognized the beneficial effects of lower prices on competition and there have been relatively few price discrimination cases. Antidumping laws have been increasingly zealous in attacking unfair foreign trade practices.

---

[22]G.N. Horlick, "The Canada-U.S. Trade Negotiations and U.S. Trade Laws: Possibilities for Reform" (Paper presented at a seminar sponsored by McCarthy & McCarthy, Toronto, January 1986).

[23]See R.H. Bork, *The Antitrust Paradox: A Policy at War with Itself* (New York: Basic Books, 1978); and S.C. Salop, ed., *Strategy, Predation and Antitrust Analysis* (Washington, D.C.: Federal Trade Commission, 1981).

National treatment of firms penalized for dumping or price discounting would limit the potential for discrimination between domestic and foreign firms in future. Furthermore, national treatment in price discrimination laws would not require necessarily that each country use the same criteria in applying such laws. Simple logic may not prevail however, and we now turn to a consideration of other approaches.

Revised Criteria

The second negotiating approach involves retaining bilateral antidumping mechanisms while revising the criteria by which they are applied. In particular, eliminating "sale below cost" provisions in bilateral antidumping laws would remove the most protectionist elements of such laws. Under these existing special provisions, duties may be levied even though no dumping actually occurs. Where companies are not covering their overhead costs in their home market, dumping margins are calculated on the difference between the export price and a "constructed value" based on an estimate of a price that would cover all costs and still yield a normal profit.

Eliminating "sale below cost" provisions in bilateral antidumping laws would bring those laws closer to the standard prevailing in domestic price discrimination laws and would reduce the application of antidumping duties as well as the number of complaints and investigations. At the same time, the incidence of dumping could be reduced by a "boomerang" provision, whereby companies selling a product in the other country cannot prevent, and the originating country must facilitate, the re-export of the product to the producing firms' domestic market.[24] The boomerang provision is one aspect of the European Free Trade Association's (EFTA) rules of competition that could be relevant to the Canadian-U.S. negotiations.

The revised criteria approach is administratively more complicated and lacks the protection against potential abuses of antidumping measures that the national treatment approach provides. However, some may consider it to be an attractive negotiating route because it would avoid the perception that the antidumping system was being dismantled. If antidumping duties were likely to be applied only rarely once tariffs were eliminated, then retaining such mechanisms for bilateral trade could be a relatively costless way to reassure domestic firms that fear being overwhelmed by the reduction of

---

[24]J.S. Lambrinidis, *The Structure, Function and Law of a Free Trade Area: The European Free Trade Association* (New York: Praeger, 1965), p. 149.

bilateral trade barriers. The risk would still remain, however, that administrative and judicial interpretation of antidumping laws could be subject to a protectionist bias in either or both countries.

Joint Administration

The third possible negotiating approach would involve some form of joint administration of bilateral import relief laws. Joint administration could involve a relatively loose arrangement requiring formal consultation between the two countries before bilateral antidumping duties are imposed. Alternatively, it could involve some variation on the proposal made by the Royal Commission on the Economic Union and Development Prospects for Canada (the Macdonald Commission) to have import relief laws administered by a binational tribunal.

Before examining these alternative approaches, it is important to distinguish between the processes available to industries in either country to seek redress from import competition and the mechanisms for settling disputes between governments that could be developed as part of a bilateral agreement. A bilateral agreement almost certainly will create an intergovernmental dispute settlement mechanism, but this mechanism may not replace existing national import relief systems. Nonetheless, developing this type of intergovernmental machinery could help defuse and resolve disputes that now tend to be dealt with under import relief laws.

The looser arrangement requiring consultation between governments before antidumping duties are imposed is the approach taken in agreements between the EC and EFTA.[25] In the case of these agreements, the consultative approach seems to resolve many of the disputes arising from allegations of dumping, but that is because the domestic administration of these countries' antidumping systems allows room for government discretion. The mandatory quasi-judicial features of the U.S. system allow for less discretion. (The Canadian system is now similar to the U.S. system in its use of a quasi-judicial process to determine injury. The imposition of duties is not legally mandatory in Canadian law, but duties are imposed in virtually all cases where injury is found.) Thus, the consultative approach to joint administration is unlikely to be appropriate for the Canadian and U.S. trade law systems.

The Macdonald Commission's proposal responds to the more formal nondiscretionary import regulatory systems that exist in the

---

[25]See, for example, Articles 25 and 27, Agreement between the European Economic Community and the Kingdom of Sweden, December 1972.

two countries. Such a proposal could provide an administrative process to deal with bilateral trade disputes; indeed, some observers perceive it to be a panacea for bilateral irritants. Some important questions would need to be resolved, however. If, for example, the legislative criteria for applying bilateral antidumping duties remain unchanged, it is argued, binational administration then would be more impartial. Others, however, might regard the transfer of injury determinations to a joint tribunal as a transfer of sovereignty.

Procedural Changes

The fourth approach involves retaining separate national antidumping systems but changing domestic procedures and standards for injury determination. One proposed procedural change would separate Canadian imports into the United States (or U.S. imports into Canada) from third-country imports in the application of antidumping duties, thereby reducing the likelihood that such duties would be applied to bilateral trade. Although Canadian exporters still could be subject to the cost of investigations, it would remove the present incentives to include Canadian imports in complaints about imports from third countries in order to improve the likelihood of an injury determination. Such a procedural change could be difficult to negotiate, however, since segregating imports runs contrary to recent developments in U.S. trade law. Under the *Trade and Tariff Act of 1984*, for instance, imports from several countries are cumulated to determine injury.

The injury test itself is sufficiently subjective and fluid that there might be a spate of antidumping and countervailing duties, even under this segregated approach, if the administrative criteria for injury determination were relaxed. To avoid this potential abuse of the system, more specific injury standards could be negotiated for the bilateral agreement. In particular, tighter standards of injury for the preliminary determination could reduce the potential for harassment through the launching of spurious actions.[26] A related proposal involves implementing a requirement that there be a stricter causal link between injury, the margin of dumping, and import volumes in the two countries' domestic import regulation systems.[27]

---

[26]Horlick, "The Canada-U.S. Trade Negotiations."

[27]D. Steger, "The Impact of U.S. Trade Laws on Canadian Economic Policies", in C.D. Howe Institute, *Policy Harmonization: The Effects of a Canadian-American Free Trade Area* (Toronto, 1986), pp. 73–100.

Table 3
U.S. Countervailing Duty Investigations
of Canadian Exports, 1980–86

Year	Product	Injury finding	Subsidy ruling
1980	frozen potato products	negative	—
	unprepared fish	negative, preliminary	negative; dismissed
	potassium chloride (review investigation)	negative	—
1981	herring fillets	—	—
1982	softwood products	affirmative, preliminary	negative; dismissed
	rail passenger cars	affirmative	terminated (petition withdrawn)
1984	hogs and pork	hogs, affirmative; pork, negative	affirmative; hogs 4.39¢/lb.
1985	fresh Atlantic groundfish	affirmative	affirmative; 5.82% duty
	iron & steel, pipes & tubes	affirmative	negative
	raspberries	—	government negotiations terminated
	gas and oilwell tubular steel products	affirmative	affirmative; 0.72% duty
1986	softwood lumber	affirmative	affirmative
	carnations	affirmative	affirmative

Sources: United States, International Trade Commission, *Annual Report*, various issues; and United States, Office of the U.S. Trade Representative, *Annual Report of the President on the Trade Agreements Program*, various issues.

Subsidies

Although government subsidies, such as financing the construction of railways and canals, have affected Canadian-U.S. trade since the nineteenth century, they have become a bilateral trade issue only within the past 15 years. Prior to the 1970s, the two countries shared a postwar consensus that export subsidies should be prohibited. Since neither country provided significant export subsidies, the issue of countervailing duties directed against such subsidies was largely irrelevant to bilateral trade. One exception, in the early 1960s, involved a U.S. radiator manufacturer's allegation that Canada's automotive duty remission scheme constituted an export subsidy. Since there was no requirement for an injury finding in U.S. countervailing duty law at that time, duties likely would have been imposed on automotive products from Canada. But this dispute was resolved by the negotiation of the Canadian-U.S. auto pact in 1965, which provided for bilateral duty-free trade.

The 1973 U.S. Michelin tire decision was the first example of the imposition of countervailing duties on products receiving domestic subsidies. Although other U.S. countervailing duty cases were launched against Canadian products in the 1970s, the effects of such actions on bilateral trade were limited by the U.S. waiver of countervailing duties for countries participating in the Tokyo Round of trade negotiations under a special provision of the *Trade Act of 1974.*

The conclusion of the Tokyo Round ushered in a new era in the administration of countervailing duties, with significant implications for bilateral trade. On the U.S. side, there have been 13 countervailing duty investigations on Canadian products since 1980, as shown in Table 3. Six of these actions were unsuccessful, two were resolved by negotiations, three resulted in duties, and two are still unresolved. On the Canadian side, countervailing duty legislation providing recourse for private petitioners has been operative only since the passage of the *Special Import Measures Act* in 1984. A Canadian countervailing duty investigation of U.S. corn exports is currently under way, while Revenue Canada has issued a preliminary ruling of subsidy in the amount of 67 percent.

The effects of subsidies on trade and the application of countervailing duties by national governments are among the most controversial trade issues of the 1980s. In the absence of clear multilateral rules, countries are acting unilaterally. As Aho and Aronson observe:

> Subsidies and to a lesser extent government procurement go to the heart of the fairness question, but it is difficult to measure the extent to which they distort trade. It is an empirical question how much subsidies imposed for domestic purposes distort trade and injure foreign countries. More difficult still is the extent to which subsidies for R&D or preferential government treatment may create a permanent advantage for an industry. Lacking a multilateral agreement on what practices are unfair, countries (especially the United States) are unilaterally defining unfairness and, when they consider it legitimate, impose countervailing duties.[28]

National Treatment

National treatment raises particularly difficult problems on subsidy issues because neither country has domestic mechanisms to discipline the use and effects of subsidies by various levels of government. In principle, one can argue that subsidies are constrained by government budgets and that governments should be free to engage in domestic subsidies. Yet U.S. import-competing interests, as well as Congress, are unlikely to accept this position, because the

---

[28]C.M. Aho and J.D. Aronson, *Trade Talks: America Better Listen* (New York: Council on Foreign Relations, 1985), p. 50.

prospect of U.S. firms competing with foreign treasuries appears to them to be inherently unfair and raises the specter of government-supported predatory behavior. Of course, Canadian farmers have similar sentiments regarding the global subsidy war in agriculture, and more Canadian industries may adopt a similar view as they become familiar with the application of Canada's new countervailing duty laws.

Obtaining a bilateral exemption from the application of countervailing duties would require both governments to pledge to limit the use of subsidies. Uncertainties exist, however, about the commitment each government would be willing to make (and stick to) about its subsidy practices in order for the other government to exempt it from the application of countervailing duties. The approach the Canadian-American Committee suggested in its 1965 proposal for a Canadian-U.S. Free Trade Area was that "the partners will identify those government aids obviously requiring control and the appropriate method of neutralizing their discriminatory effects."[29] Pledging to dismantle voluntarily subsidy programs that distort trade is the approach taken in the EC-EFTA agreements.[30] In those agreements, the parties retain the right to impose countervailing duties on an FTA partner, although the countervailing duty provisions are rarely invoked. The EC itself, which does not permit countervailing duties on trade among member countries, uses a somewhat different approach involving a complex supranational regulatory and legal system intended to control the subsidy practices of its members.

A basis for applying national treatment to bilateral trade would be an effective Canadian-U.S. mechanism to discipline and disallow subsidy programs. Such a mechanism could be a better way to deal with bidding rivalries among governments seeking to attract new investment projects. Although controls on these bidding wars would be desirable, U.S. and Canadian legislators likely would be reluctant to cede sovereignty to a supranational agency or tribunal that would have the power to disallow domestic spending programs. Yet, in the absence of such a mechanism, it is going to be very difficult to obtain legislative approval for the national treatment option regarding countervailing duties.

Nonetheless, opening borders and reducing or eliminating non-tariff barriers does serve to constrain the effects of subsidies and

---

[29]Canadian-American Committee, *A Possible Plan for A Canada-U.S. Free Trade Area* (Washington, D.C.; Montreal: Canadian-American Committee, 1965), p. 8.
[30]See Article 23 (iii), Agreement between the European Economic Community and the Kingdom of Sweden, December 1972.

to undermine the rationale for the application of countervailing duties. As was noted previously, open borders limit the ability of governments to underwrite the losses of firms. Also, liberalization of export controls on primary resource products removes the potential for differences in natural resource policies to have any effect on trade in processed resource products. Thus, an EFTA agreement does provide a rationale either for a national treatment approach to, or for substantial clarification of the definition of, subsidies.

Revised Criteria

A revised definition of a countervailable subsidy could provide greater certainty to producers in one country exporting to the other. One approach is to take seriously the metaphor of the "level playing field", in the sense of focusing on practices that significantly affect the pattern of trade.[31] The objective would be to distinguish between those subsidies that distort trade and those that do not.

This objective is quite consistent with previously stated U.S. positions on subsidies. At the outset of the Tokyo Round, the United States sought to distinguish between three categories of subsidies. It wanted the first category, explicit export subsidies, to be prohibited under the GATT and to be subject to countervailing duties without requiring a determination of injury. It wanted the second category, domestic subsidies that have a significant effect on trade, to be subject to countervailing duties if they were found to be causing material injury to a domestic industry. The third category would have consisted of permitted domestic subsidies with only indirect effects on trade, which would not have been subject to countervailing duties.[32] The United States did not achieve its objective but instead agreed to the compromise embodied in the Tokyo Round Subsidies Code. As a result, the United States implemented the injury test for all foreign subsidies and the issue of determining the trade effects of subsidies was left unresolved.

Current U.S. countervailing duty law does not attempt to categorize different types of subsidies or to examine whether they distort trade. Instead, the issue of whether domestic subsidies are countervailable depends on the legal interpretation of whether or not the subsidy is specific.

The principle of distinguishing between specific and general subsidies is clear. As Hufbauer and Erb state:

---

[31]Lipsey and Smith, *Taking the Initiative*, p. 144.
[32]C. Pestieau, *Subsidies and Countervailing Duties: The Negotiating Issues* (Montreal: C.D. Howe Research Institute, 1976), pp. 14–19.

[G]overnments should be free to offer general incentives to industry or agriculture — for example, by way of tax relief, roads, ports,
or schools — but governments should not offer sector-specific incentives that injuriously affect the commerce of another nation.[33]

The rationale for distinguishing between the two types of subsidies is that the former may distort trade, while the latter will not
because adjustment in the exchange rate will absorb most or all of
the effects on the international competitive position of individual
industries.[34]

A serious practical difficulty with the specificity concept is that
while it may be desirable to distinguish between specific and general
subsidies, it is very difficult to do so. In its rulings, for example,
the ITA has found consistently that subsidies available to the entire agricultural sector are not subject to countervailing duties, while
programs that for administrative reasons are differentiated by com-
modity groups are countervailable.[35]

In its 1986 preliminary ruling on softwood lumber, the ITA in-
terpreted specificity criteria in terms of the number of industries
that have access to a government program. On that basis, the ITA
concluded stumpage subsidies to be countervailable because the
principal purchasers of public timber in Canada are the sawmill and
pulp and paper industries, and those two industries are highly in-
tegrated. Economic criteria for the specificity test would focus on
the share of the total trade accounted for by a group of industries,
not an arbitrary determination of the number of industries. Yet between them, the sawmill, pulp and paper, and other wood products
industries account for a much larger share of Canadian exports than
does agriculture. It is inconsistent for the ITA to determine that
programs available to agriculture are not countervailable but that
those available to the forestry sector are.

Another reason cited by the ITA in overturning the 1983 softwood
lumber decision is its allegation that provincial governments exer-
cise discretion in the allocation of timber leases. This reasoning ex-
pands substantially the range of government practices and public
policies that might be considered to be countervailable subsidies.
Under this new doctrine, the administration of regulations governing hazardous wastes or the allocation of pollution rights could be

---

[33]Hufbauer and Erb, *Subsidies in International Trade*, p. 11.
[34]This argument is an extension of the border tax adjustment issue. See H. Johnson
and M. Krauss, "Border Taxes, Border Tax Adjustments, Comparative Advantage,
and the Balance of Payments," *Canadian Journal of Economics* 3 (1970): 595–602;
and Hufbauer and Erb, *Subsidies in International Trade*, pp. 51–56.
[35]Steger, "The Impact of U.S. Trade Laws."

regarded as a subsidy to the chemical industry or other basic industries. Other government policies, such as assistance for research and development, which formerly would have been regarded as widely available, could now be treated as a countervailable subsidy.

The softwood lumber ruling did not consider the central issue of whether differences in Canadian and U.S. timber leasing and stumpage appraisal systems actually have any distorting effect on trade. Some economists have argued that such differences do not distort trade.[36] No doubt the U.S. petitioner would argue the contrary.

The softwood lumber case is highly contentious, but the point of the discussion should be clear. Presumably, the purpose of countervailing duties is to counteract subsidies that distort international trade. One way to implement this principle would be to apply duties only to the differential between subsidies available to firms in one country and those available to similar firms in the other country. At present, Canadian goods can be subject to U.S. countervailing duties if they receive a subsidy in Canada, even if competing U.S. firms receive an equivalent or greater subsidy from U.S. federal or state governments. U.S. goods are subject to similar treatment in Canada.

Focusing on trade-distorting practices would require that countervailing duties be considered only when it is shown that the imported goods received a larger subsidy than was available to domestic producers. This suggestion could be implemented in a number of different ways. One way is to pass legislation preventing the initiation of cases where the industry on both sides of the border was subsidized. Another, perhaps more acceptable, route is to apply the *de minimis* subsidy level to the subsidy differential, not the foreign subsidy. (Under current U.S. law, *de minimis* subsidies are those that are less than one-half of 1 percent of the sale value of the product.) Calculating the net differential subsidy, however, would be complex to administer. Another approach, which would have similar effects but which would be easier to administer, is to permit a higher threshold level of subsidies that are *de minimis*, since subsidies as low as 0.5 percent do not significantly affect international trade flows.

Regional subsidies also could be permitted if they did not alter international trade patterns. In the negotiations, Canada seeks to reserve the right to subsidize lower-income, higher-cost regions as a matter of national policy. The effectiveness of such Canadian policies could be enhanced, while retaining disciplines on the extent to which they are used, by permitting cost offsets in the calculation

---

[36]See, for example, M.B. Percy, *Forest Management and Economic Growth in British Columbia* (Ottawa: Economic Council of Canada, 1986).

of countervailing duties or regional subsidies. The argument here
is that while it should be of no concern to the United States if Canadians elect to lower their average standard of living by directing
production away from lowest-cost locations, Canadian subsidies
should not be allowed to reduce the costs of Canadian firms below
those that would have been determined in a free market. This approach also may be hard to administer because of the difficulty in
determining the extent to which the displacement of production occurs within Canada or across the Canadian-U.S. border, especially
when trade barriers have been eliminated.

Another way to distinguish between subsidies that affect trade
and those that do not could be to negotiate a list of acceptable subsidies that would not be liable to countervailing duties as long as
they do not exceed a threshold level. Provincial and state governments would have to list all their current subsidy policies. New subsidies then could be added subsequently, or the level of subsidies
under existing programs could be increased, but only by mutual
agreement. In this way, the two countries could be assured that
provincial and state policies do not provide for ever-increasing subsidization. Such an approach would restrain self-defeating, beggar-
thy-neighbor state and provincial development policies — at least
those that employ subsidies. Having an agreed list of subsidies
would assure provincial and state governments, and the firms and
workers they wish to help, that those subsidies would not attract
countervailing duty investigations — especially after firms had accepted the subsidies and based their investment decisions on them.

Even if it were possible to agree on only a few types of mutually
acceptable subsidies, this could still remove existing ambiguities.
Subsidies to improve environmental quality or occupational health,
for example, could be exempted from countervailing procedures. At
present, a Canadian smelter receiving a government subsidy to in-
stall a scrubber intended to reduce pollution, including transboun-
dary pollution, could be subject to U.S. countervailing duties on its
output because the Canadian government has "assumed a cost" of
production.

Another approach would be to negotiate an exhaustive list of ac-
tionable subsidies potentially subject to duties. If governments introduced new subsidy programs, there could be preclearance to
determine whether those subsidies are countervailable. This would
provide governments in both countries with a clear indication of the
risks of pursuing subsidy policies. It would also prevent private petitioners from alleging that any and every government policy or practice constitutes a subsidy, and it would provide greater certainty
for exporters. The regulatory authority that administers the coun-

tervailing duty law would be instructed not to accept a private-sector petition unless it alleged subsidies that were on the list of those that were agreed to be countervailable. Not only would this reduce the potential for harassment by private petitioners, but it would help prevent changes in the administrative and judicial interpretation of the law resulting in further broadening the types of government policies that were considered to be countervailable subsidies.

Efforts are now under way to broaden the application of counter-vailing duties to ephemeral "subsidies" in the form of differences in national regulatory systems or targeting practices, in addition to the more prosaic subsidies in the form of government payments and special tax incentives. In light of such efforts, petitioners could be required to demonstrate that the alleged practice actually had a significant effect on the pattern of trade before it could be added to the list of countervailable subsidies. An alternative proposal along these lines is to preclude the application of countervailing duties if the exporting country can demonstrate that the alleged subsidy does not alter trade patterns.[37]

Finally, there is considerable scope for both countries to agree on the precise methods of calculating subsidies. As an ITA ruling states:

> We have considerable latitude to calculate the value of subsidy....In our opinion, all that is required of us is that the methods we adopt be reasonable.[38]

The issue of calculation of a subsidy can be highly contentious. When the ITA made its softwood lumber ruling, for example — and quite apart from the issue of whether stumpage practices are a subsidy — Canada alleged that it had double counted by adding the imputed cost of producing standing timber to an estimate of the imputed value of the timber.

Although this discussion has focused on issues surrounding U.S. countervailing duty laws, negotiations on the definition of subsidies would serve to clarify Canada's countervailing duty laws as well. Canada's 1984 *Special Import Measures Act* has the following very broad definition:

> '[S]ubsidy' includes any financial or other commercial benefit that has accrued or will accrue, directly or indirectly, to persons engaged

---

[37]See J. Barcelo, "Subsidies and Countervailing Duties — Analysis and Proposal," *Law and Policy in International Business* 9 (1977): 851.

[38]United States, International Trade Administration, "Subsidies Appendix to Cold-Rolled Carbon Steel Products," *Federal Register*, 1984, p. 18016.

in the production, manufacture, growth, processing, purchase, dis-
tribution, transportation, sale, export or import of goods, as a result
of any scheme, program, practice or thing done, provided or implemented by the government of a country other than Canada, but
does not include the amount of any duty or internal tax imposed
on goods by the government of the country of origin or country
of export from which the goods, because of their exportation from
the country of export or country of origin, have been exempted
or have been or will be relieved by means of refund or drawback.[39]

Canadian regulations further elaborate on this broad definition. And
in the decision on imports of U.S. corn, Canadian authorities have
applied a stricter version of the specificity test than has the United
States in its recent decisions. Regulations and administrative practices are changed easily, however, and the Canadian definition of subsidies subject to countervailing duties could be broadened in future.

As Canadian industries become familiar with Canada's new countervailing duty laws, more countervailing duty actions could occur
in future. Thus, a more precise definition of subsidies in Canadian
law would help prevent bilateral frictions. Although Canadian countervailing duty actions will not have the same effect on U.S.
producers as when applied in reverse, the application of Canadian
countervailing duties to U.S. products could stimulate other countries to take similar actions.

Joint Administration

The regulatory procedures governing the application of countervailing duties correspond closely to those pertaining to antidumping. Thus, the earlier discussion of possible joint administration of
the antidumping system also applies to countervailing duties directed against subsidies. In light of U.S. sensitivities about subsidies
and countervailing duties, the U.S. government is likely to be reluctant to surrender the administration of countervailing duty laws
to a binational agency, particularly for making determinations of
injury. Nonetheless, a joint mechanism for investigating and measur-
ing subsidy practices as provided for in the substantive provisions
of the bilateral trade agreement could be very useful in identifying
the effects of subsidies on trade. For example, the proposal to impose countervailing duties on the subsidy differential would require
joint administration of the measurement of the subsidy.

Revised Procedures

Through this negotiating approach, the possible revisions to

---

[39]Canada, *Special Import Measures Act*, 1984, Section 2 (1).

domestic regulatory procedures governing the application of antidumping duties that were discussed earlier also could apply to countervailing duties. Requiring petitioners to demonstrate a causal link between a subsidy practice and injury would be a significant change from current Canadian and U.S. procedures. If adopted, proposals to define injury standards more clearly and to refine the procedures for investigating bilateral countervailing duty cases would limit some of the potential abuses of countervailing duty laws, since those laws presumably are directed against subsidies that actually distort international trade.

Import Disruption

In the preceding sections, the rationale for import relief measures rests on allegations of unfair trade practices. When it comes to import competition, however, the issue is different because there have been no allegations of unfair conduct in this case. Canada and the United States both have "safeguard" or "escape clause" provisions in their import relief laws. Under these provisions, import quotas or tariff surcharges can be applied when surges in imports result in "serious injury" to domestic producers, the definition of which is based on a stricter standard than "material injury".

Special safeguard provisions apply to agricultural products, notably Section 22 of the U.S. *Agricultural Adjustment Act of 1933* and Canada's "fast-track" surtax provisions on horticultural products. Since agricultural trade raises special issues, and since commodities subject to marketing board regulations or price supports may not be brought under the agreement, these particular provisions are not discussed in this paper.

Until recently, both countries have sought to use policy discretion to limit the bilateral application of escape clause measures, at least in the case of trade in industrial products. The recent increase in bilateral safeguard actions is a result of increased U.S. protectionism. This in turn is the result of excess capacity and low prices in many industries, due, to a considerable degree, to the overvalued U.S. dollar. But these pressures have historical antecedents, as the following comment on the U.S. *Trade Expansion Act of 1962* suggests.

> Specific differences between the old and new escape authority were outlined by Tariff Commission Chairman Ben D. Dorfman in his opening statement before the softwood lumber hearing on October 2, 1962. The new legislation may tend to simplify and clarify the criteria for making a determination of injury.

- Under the old legislation, the increased imports could be either 'actual' or 'relative' to domestic production; the 1962 Act makes no such distinction.
- Previously, the Tariff Commission had been required to determine whether increased imports causing or threatening serious injury to a domestic industry resulted 'in whole or in part' from the 'duty or other customs treatment reflecting' a trade agreement concession. Now, the Tariff Commission can make a simpler determination: whether the allegedly injurious increased imports result 'in major part' from 'concessions granted under trade agreements.'
- The new legislation omits reference to the specific injury factors enumerated in Section 7 of the 1951 Act, but provides that the Commission is to 'take into account all economic factors which it considers relevant, including idling of productive facilities, inability to operate at a level of reasonable profit, and unemployment or underemployment.'
- Under the old law, the increased imports must 'have contributed substantially towards causing or threatening serious injury to such industry'....The corresponding clause in the 1962 legislation provides a more precise criterion: such increased imports must be 'the major factor in causing, or threatening to cause, such injury.'[40]

The net effect of the changes to the escape clause provision incorporated in the 1962 act and in those of 1951, 1955, and 1958 was to increase the likelihood that industries or firms would qualify for assistance measures. In this respect, the effect of these acts could be viewed as trade restricting, not trade expanding. But an important innovation in the 1962 act was to offer the administration the choice of providing import relief in the form of tariff surcharges or quotas, or, instead, providing adjustment assistance for firms — such as loans for restructuring — or for workers — such as supplemental unemployment insurance and retraining or relocation assistance.

The U.S. *Trade Act of 1974* continued the trend of these earlier acts by widening the eligibility of firms to claim relief from import competition under the escape clause provision. It dropped the required link between a negotiated reduction in trade barriers and an increase in imports. Since the president retained discretion to reject or vary the International Trade Commission's (ITC) recommendations for import relief, however, the effects of this wider eligibility for import relief now depend on the administration's conduct of trade policy.

On the Canadian side, legal provisions permitting safeguards, as they apply to bilateral trade, have evolved more slowly. Unlike in

---

[40]F. Masson and H.E. English, *Invisible Trade Barriers Between Canada and the United States* (Washington, D.C.; Montreal: Canadian-American Committee, 1963), p. 28.

the United States, private parties cannot initiate such actions under Canadian law. Instead, Canadians must request that the government consider launching an investigation.

Canada has developed a special trade regime for textiles and apparel under the aegis of the Textile and Clothing Board, a separate agency from the Canadian Import Tribunal. As a result, orderly marketing arrangements covering an ever-widening range of products in this sector have been negotiated with an expanding number of low-cost supplier countries. Bilateral trade in textiles and clothing is restricted at present only by the high tariffs both countries have erected.

Yet, safeguard measures have tended to cause bilateral difficulties because of problems both countries have experienced with imports from offshore producers. In 1976, for example, Canada imposed global quotas on apparel and in 1977 took similar action on footwear. Both actions had only small adverse effects on U.S. exports because most imports came from offshore. Quotas on apparel were removed shortly thereafter as new orderly marketing arrangements were negotiated with offshore producers, but quotas on footwear were not lifted until 1985 and were a continuing bilateral irritant.

On the U.S. side, there have been several escape clause investigations involving Canadian products in the 1980s, as shown in Table 4. In 1983, for example, the United States imposed duties and quotas on specialty steel, which adversely affected Canadian exports of that product. Canada then invoked its rights under the GATT and retaliated on U.S. specialty steel exports. The dispute finally was settled through bilateral negotiations.

The U.S. carbon steel escape clause investigation in 1984 involved higher stakes: bilateral trade worth about Can.$2 billion. Formally at least, Canada was exempted from U.S. efforts to negotiate orderly marketing arrangements with supplier countries. But the Office of the U.S. Trade Representative has complained periodically that Canadian steel producers are not abiding by an informal commitment to be prudent in their exports to the U.S. market.

A notable exception to the rule that safeguard actions have arisen in response to offshore imports is the notorious incident involving cedar shakes and shingles. In 1986, the president accepted the ITC's recommendation and, under the escape clause provision, imposed a duty of 35 percent on cedar shakes and shingles from Canada — a product that had been duty free since a bilateral treaty of 1935. In light of this incident and other recent bilateral difficulties, good will between the two federal governments no longer seems sufficient to avoid problems arising from the bilateral application of escape clause or safeguard actions.

Table 4
U.S. Escape Clause Actions on Canadian Products, 1982–85

Year	Product	Injury finding	Presidential action
1982	carbon and certain alloy steel products	affirmative	voluntary export restraints (VERs)
1983	specialty steel products	affirmative	quotas & duties
1984	copper	affirmative	no action
	carbon steel	affirmative	VER[a]
1985	softwood shingles and shakes	affirmative	initial 35% duty
	castings	negative	—

[a] Canada was formally excluded from the bilateral restraint program, but Canadian steel producers have been enjoined to exhibit prudence in shipments to the United States.

Sources: United States, International Trade Commission, *Annual Report*, various issues; and United States, Office of the U.S. Trade Representative, *Annual Report of the President on the Trade Agreements Program*, various issues.

Conflicting considerations must be weighed in assessing the options for dealing with disruptive import surges of goods that are recognized to be fairly traded. In its look at escape clause, or safeguard, measures, the Macdonald Commission expressed the following views:

> One can argue that the preferred solution would be the complete dismantling of safeguard protection applicable to goods originating in either country. The main purpose of a free-trade arrangement's guarantee of market access may well be to create positive incentives for the parties to undertake industrial restructuring. In this instance, the continued availability of safeguard protection to firms injured by imports would substantially undermine the economic goal of the signatories. On the other hand, a free-trade agreement which offered no prospect of escape for injured domestic industries would probably attract substantial political opposition in both nations. An alternative to a complete dismantling of protection is to draft a rule providing that only if Canadian exports were found to be the primary cause of serious injury to U.S. competitors would the safeguard action apply to Canadian producers. Another possibility would be to retain safeguard measures, but to transfer the responsibility for their enforcement...to a transnational panel or tribunal created by the free-trade agreement.[41]

The Macdonald Commission touched on most of the negotiating approaches discussed here.

---

[41]Canada, Royal Commission on the Economic Union and Development Prospects for Canada, *Report*, Vol. 1 (Ottawa: Supply and Services Canada, 1985), p. 315.

National Treatment

The first approach suggested in the passage quoted above corresponds to the national treatment option, which would involve eliminating the bilateral application of safeguard measures. Each country could offer domestic assistance measures to injured firms and displaced workers — subject to whatever arrangements are made regarding subsidies and countervailing duties. But neither country could impose import quotas or tariffs on products originating in the other country in cases involving import surges. Although an economic case can be made for permitting such untrammeled competition, the opposition is likely to be political, as the quote suggests. Obtaining acceptance for this approach would require that adjustment assistance programs for displaced workers be credible and effective.[42]

Revised Criteria

The second approach involves negotiating specific criteria for the bilateral application of import measures designed to deal with disruptive imports. One proposal suggests that the two countries exempt each other from the application of escape clause measures when neither country is the principal supplier of a product that disrupts domestic industry. In the event that either country is the principal supplier of such a product, the only remedy permitted should be to raise the bilateral tariff to the most-favored-nation level. Furthermore, safeguard measures should be subject to a commitment that they will be phased out.[43]

There is a variation on the second approach that eventually would achieve the same results as would be obtained under the national treatment approach. This involves restoring the requirement that import relief under the escape clause be permitted only when the import surge is the direct result of reduced bilateral trade barriers and when the only remedy is to reverse the recent tariff concession. This type of arrangement is incorporated in the FTA arrangement between Australia and New Zealand, which provides for temporary import relief from import surges during the transition period when bilateral trade barriers are being reduced but disallows such import

---

[42]The introduction of adjustment assistance measures as a remedy for import competition would be a useful reform in the Canadian laws and procedures. See M.M. Hart, *Canadian Economic Development and the International Trading System: Constraints and Opportunities*, Collected Reseach Studies of the Royal Commission on the Economic Union and Development Prospects for Canada no. 53 (Toronto: University of Toronto Press, 1985), p. 103.

[43]Lipsey and Smith, *Taking the Initiative*, p. 159.

barriers once the agreement has been fully implemented. This latter approach would have prevented the application of duties on cedar shakes and shingles.

Joint Administration

Since safeguard actions leave more discretion to trade policymakers in both governments, the requirement to consult before applying bilateral safeguard measures is more feasible than in the case of antidumping and countervailing duties. Indeed, the FTA agreement between the United States and Israel provides for prior consultation before implementing escape clause measures. For that matter, the United States and Canada already have a bilateral arrangement calling for prior consultation on safeguard measures. Such a commitment seems unlikely to be a satisfactory solution, however, in light of recent bilateral differences over shakes and shingles and U.S. legislative proposals to limit presidential discretion in the administration of the escape clause provision.[44]

Revised Procedures

The remaining negotiating approach involves altering the standards and procedures for injury determination under the existing national systems of administration of safeguard laws. In particular, it could be useful to require that bilateral imports be the "principal cause" of "serious injury" before bilateral safeguard measures are applied. It is worth noting, however, that this proposal would not have prevented the shakes and shingles action.

Although pressures from import-competing industries are frequently strong, safeguard actions are not imbued with the rhetoric of unfair trade. Indeed, the U.S.-Israeli agreement provides for special procedures for bilateral safeguards and permits exemption of bilateral trade from measures directed at third countries. Since other barriers to competition between Canada and the United States are being removed, it may be possible to gain acceptance for limiting the bilateral application of safeguard measures, at least when the agreement is fully implemented, as part of an overall thrust to open markets.

---

[44]The omnibus trade bill in the 99th Congress would have limited sharply presidential discretion in the administration of the escape clause. The proposal to replace orderly marketing arrangements or quotas with temporary import duties as a response to import disruption has been supported by G. Hufbauer and J. Schott, *Trading for Growth: The Next Round of Trade Negotiations* (Washington, D.C.: Institute for International Economics, 1985); and R. Lawrence and R. Litan, *Saving Free Trade* (Washington, D.C.: Brookings Institution, 1985).

Linkage with the Multilateral Process

In considering the relationship between a bilateral agreement on trade laws and existing multilateral agreements, the first point that must be made is that if the agreement is part of an FTA agreement under Article XXIV of the GATT, then the two countries are largely unconstrained in the form or structure of bilateral import relief arrangements. Nonetheless, subtle interactions are possible between the design of the bilateral arrangement and the forthcoming multilateral negotiations.

The four negotiating approaches could have quite different implications for the multilateral talks. If the national treatment option were adopted for dumping or subsidies, for example, it is extremely unlikely that this option would be available to other countries unless they also wished to enter into the FTA agreement. Yet, if the approach adopted on these key problems involves retaining each country's import relief system while refining the criteria for bilateral application of antidumping and countervailing duties or escape clause measures, then other countries could press to have the same refined criteria apply to them. If the bilateral agreement involves the removal of "sales below cost" provisions in the antidumping laws, for example, other countries might seek to incorporate this approach in the GATT Antidumping Code, although they might be reluctant to take the same approach in their own antidumping laws. Similarly, if a bilateral agreement yields a more precise agreement of which subsidies are specific and thus countervailable, then other countries almost certainly will press for incorporation of more definitive criteria in the GATT Subsidies Code.

The approaches taken to the procedural issues also will affect the feasibility of subsequent broader application of the bilateral arrangements. Joint administration is not likely to be amenable to broader application, but revision of procedures for determinations of injury in the import relief laws could be incorporated quite easily in subsequent multilateral agreements dealing with dumping, subsidies, and import disruption.

It is evident that the potential extension of some of the bilateral arrangements to other countries would not be automatic and would occur through negotiations in the multilateral talks. Yet the possibility that some of the bilateral arrangements subsequently might be incorporated in plurilateral or multilateral agreements is an important strategic consideration.

In light of the potential broader application of some of the bilateral arrangements pertaining to import relief laws, import-competing interests in both countries, which initially might resist changes in such laws, also may prefer approaches that are tailored to the Canadian-U.S. relationship. As a result, these interests may become more amenable to elaboration of an entirely separate set of bilateral rules and procedures for import relief measures, which could involve a more complete overhaul or dismantling of the existing bilateral systems.

At the same time, both countries may wish to incorporate provisions into the bilateral agreement that are amenable to subsequent broader application, as part of their negotiating strategy for the multilateral trade talks. Other countries could qualify for the more precise application of import relief laws if they were prepared to liberalize their tariff and nontariff barriers to trade. In this way, bilateral negotiations of import relief laws could shape the agenda for multilateral negotiation of these issues.

Assessing the Negotiating Approaches

The four negotiating approaches could be used in different combinations and to varying degrees for each of the major trade problems. As a result, there are many potential outcomes to the bilateral negotiation of import relief laws. While this complexity makes the negotiators' task technically more demanding, it also provides them with more room to maneuver in seeking mutually satisfactory rules and procedures for bilateral trade.

The national treatment approach is the clearest and simplest way to deal with import relief measures in the context of an overall FTA agreement. Such an approach would be consistent with a bilateral agreement that goes further than previous FTA agreements and that provides national treatment for government procurement, trade in services, and investment policies. National treatment also might well be feasible in dealing with dumping, because each country has domestic laws dealing with unfair pricing. Dismantling bilateral safeguard mechanisms is more likely to encounter political resistance but could be acceptable in the context of an overall agreement.

The greatest difficulty with the national treatment approach arises in the use of subsidies. Unless a bilateral agreement can devise an acceptable process for controlling the use of subsidies, there is little likelihood that the U.S. Congress would accept the dismantling of the countervailing duty apparatus for bilateral trade. Applying national treatment to dumping but not to subsidies would create problems for Canada as well. If both countries dismantled their antidumping procedures but not their countervailing duty mechanisms, then Canada would be perceived to have made a much more significant concession than the United States.

Negotiating the criteria for application of import relief laws offers promise for improvement of all three trade problems. Clearer and more refined standards for antidumping and countervailing duties would prevent the abuse of those particular import relief measures and provide greater certainty for the public and private sectors. The principle would be to focus on those practices that are genuinely likely to be trade distorting. Similarly, requiring a close link between the recent reduction of bilateral trade barriers and the application of bilateral safeguard measures would provide a safety valve for industries that might experience unanticipated difficulties adjusting to increased competition in the North American market. Such a link also would limit the potential for protectionist actions once the agreement is fully implemented.

Joint administration of bilateral import laws appears to be less of a panacea than some observers suggest. A loose arrangement involving a requirement to consult before applying bilateral import measures is incompatible with the formal quasi-judicial nature of the two countries' antidumping and countervailing duty laws. A joint tribunal and administrative agency, however, could bring an assurance of more impartiality to the administration of such laws. Although joint administrative processes might be very useful in investigating allegations of dumping and subsidies, legislators may be reluctant to yield the injury determination process to a supranational tribunal.

Revising procedures in domestic import relief systems could be useful in reducing the potential for harassment of trade between the two countries. Clarifying the standards for injury determination and the assessment of the causal links between imports, alleged dumping or subsidization, and injury to a domestic industry also could serve to limit the potential for abuse of bilateral import relief laws.

Conclusion: Achieving a Balance

Any obligations about import relief laws and procedures to which the two countries would agree in bilateral negotiations likely would be symmetric — that is, both countries would accept the same formal obligations. Nonetheless, Canada has the greater interest in obtaining more secure access to the U.S. market. Consequently, Canadian interests in constraining the application of U.S. import relief measures will have to be balanced against high-priority U.S. interests, which include eliminating higher Canadian tariffs and negotiating rules regarding trade in services, intellectual property, and investment policies.

Achieving an overall balance in a bilateral agreement is going to be a difficult task but, as the preceding discussion indicates, there are several ways to resolve this issue. The approach, or combination of approaches, that might be adopted remains uncertain at this stage. It will take hard bargaining between the two negotiating teams — each of which will be guided by consultation with the private sector and directed by their political leaders — to find an approach that is mutually acceptable. Ultimately, developing better, clearer rules for bilateral trade requires summoning the political will to focus on longer-term mutual benefits.

The chief obstacle on the U.S. side arises from resistance to negotiating trade remedy laws. This resistance, particularly with regard to laws directed against unfair trade, is likely to be intense because the specter of unfair foreign competition touches a deep chord in the American psyche, and the enormous U.S. trade deficit has aggravated Americans' concerns. With an eventual and inevitable turnaround in the U.S. trade balance as that country is obliged to service its mounting foreign debt obligations, it is in the long-term interest of the United States to take a selective, focused approach to "trade remedies". This point, however, is not widely understood. The persistence of the U.S. trade deficit in the face of the recent sharp decline in the U.S. dollar could exacerbate protectionist pressures in the near term.

While the United States may be reluctant to negotiate import relief laws, Canada may be unwilling to accept anything other than the national treatment approach. Yet, at the same time, Canadians could be reluctant to make similar concessions on issues of interest to the United States. The issue of national treatment for services industries and investment is just as sensitive for Canadians as the national treatment approach to import relief laws is for Americans.

Canada has emphasized its concerns about the "continual threat of unilateral changes in the rules of the game"[45] regarding the terms of access to the U.S. market. The United States has expressed similar concerns about Canada's tendency to change the rules unilaterally. But U.S. concerns have been greater about investment and tax policies and about intellectual property issues. While Canada's primary goal in the trade negotiations is to achieve a more open and predictable trade regime, the United States' primary goal is to secure a more open and predictable environment for investment.

Beyond the perspective of the negotiators, who must focus on the differences in national objectives, both countries stand to gain from a more predictable bilateral trade and investment climate. Firms can

---

[45]Kelleher, Report by Minister for International Trade, p. 68.

then concentrate on generating and seizing market opportunities that yield more jobs and higher incomes for citizens of both countries. The expanded trading opportunities and more secure investment climate that could flow from establishing a new set of mutually agreed rules for regulating the world's largest bilateral trade and investment relationship will enhance the capability of the highly interdependent Canadian and U.S. economies to meet global competitive challenges.

Comments

C. Michael Aho

Before making specific comments on Murray Smith's excellent paper, I would like to set the context in which any trade agreement between Canada and the United States may be struck. I will set out a series of premises and assumptions so that those who are less pessimistic than I can readily find the basis of our disagreement.

First, a trade agreement will have to be completed between now and the spring of 1988 — on Ronald Reagan's watch, if you will, and before the Mulroney government must face the Canadian electorate. There is a narrow window of opportunity for these historic talks, but if they extend beyond 1988 that window probably will be slammed shut. Already there are signs of the talks becoming a political football in Canada.

Second, the U.S. administration needs a trade bill in 1987 to extend its authority to negotiate, both bilaterally and multilaterally. The U.S. Constitution grants Congress the authority to "regulate foreign commerce" and, historically, Congress has delegated to the executive branch the authority to negotiate. The current delegation of negotiating authority expires on January 3, 1988. As it is written today, the law gives the president a broad mandate to negotiate trade agreements and requires "fast-track" consideration of those agreements by Congress within 60 legislative days with no amendments. Without an extension of "fast-track" negotiating authority, the executive branch would lack credibility in negotiating with other countries, because any agreements reached would be subject to amendments and delay.

Third, passage of a trade bill extending the authority to negotiate always comes at a price. The price paid on previous occasions, in 1962 and 1974, was that Congress rewrote U.S. trade remedy laws, included provisions for worker adjustment assistance, and gave more authority to the Office of the U.S. Trade Representative. The 1979 trade bill implementing the results of the Tokyo Round multilateral trade negotiations further expanded the reach of U.S. trade remedy laws and limited presidential discretion in cases of unfair trade practices. Any trade bill introduced in 1987 likely will continue the trend in U.S. trade remedy laws to which Smith alludes. Thus, any changes will make it easier to obtain import relief. I expect that a new bill will broaden the definition of unfair trade practices, reduce presidential discretion over whether to impose restrictions, and man-

date retaliation under certain circumstances. But these are the very
things that Canada wishes to avoid in establishing a comprehensive trade agreement with the United States.

Fourth, Canada is looking for changes in U.S. trade remedy laws
from a U.S. administration that has proven itself extremely inept
in getting its way with Congress on trade matters. After more than
four years of "malign neglect" by the administration, Congress
revolted in April 1986 and almost denied the administration the fast-
track authority to negotiate with Canada. Recall that the resolution of disapproval failed on a 10–10 tie in the Senate Finance Committee after two days of intense lobbying by President Reagan to
obtain the critical tenth vote. Congress has lost confidence in the
president's ability to conduct trade policy, and in order to get an
extension of negotiating authority, the president will have to accept
something he has found unpalatable in the past. That will almost
certainly include an expansion of the trade remedy laws as described
above.

Fifth, these historic negotiations will be extraordinarily complex.
They are trying to address the contentious trade problems of unfairness, services, intellectual property, and investment, the latter
three of which have never been negotiated successfully on an international basis. Many countries, especially the United States, have
been defining unfairness unilaterally, much to the consternation of
others. Negotiations on these matters will raise questions of national
sovereignty and will touch on national objectives other than economic efficiency — including domestic economic equity, privacy, and
national security. The complexity of these negotiations means that
they can not be conducted over a long weekend. Months of in-depth
analysis and consultation with the private sector will be necessary
before trade-offs can be explored and strategies developed. Until now,
however, preparations on the U.S. side have been negligible.

Sixth, the U.S. administration is treating these negotiations as
a distraction rather than as a potentially pathbreaking process.
Analysis is lacking, the interagency process is dormant, the private
sector has not been mobilized, and a strategy has not been developed at a political level. Given the lack of preparation and the administration's ineptness in working with Congress, these
negotiations have a high probability of failure.

Enough of the background. Suffice it to say that difficult international and domestic negotiations lie ahead. But if they can get
around to it, the negotiators should read Smith's paper, because it
lays out a schematic of the various trade remedy laws and possible
solutions to them, including providing for national treatment, changing domestic statutes, and establishing bilateral institutional solu-

tions. I will make a brief comment on each law and then return to what I find lacking in Smith's text.

With 80 percent of Canadian exports (accounting for over 20 percent of Canada's GNP) going to the United States, it is quite natural that Canada would seek assured and enhanced access to the U.S. market. But the degree of dependence is not reciprocal. Only 22 percent of U.S. exports go to Canada. In considering changes in U.S. trade remedy laws, therefore, Congress will look very carefully at the implications such changes might have on multilateral talks. To the extent that any U.S.-Canadian agreement on trade remedy laws rests on the unique nature of the bilateral relationship, it will stand a better chance of acceptance in Congress.

Of the various trade remedy laws, those on antidumping provide the best opportunity for developing the relationship, because each country has price discrimination statutes. National treatment is a possibility, because both countries could use the price discrimination statutes to address alleged dumping. But this would require some harmonization, or at least modification, of the price discrimination statutes over time and an agreement by the United States not to resort to dumping statutes that are based on average, not marginal, costs.

National treatment is not likely on subsidies and countervailing duties, because neither country's federal government has jurisdiction over the practices of subnational governments. Subsidies go to the heart of the unfairness problem. There is no agreement over what constitutes a subsidy. Furthermore, the extent to which "domestic" subsidies or economic policies affect trade flows and injure parties in other countries is an empirical question on which reasonable people could disagree. Congress is unlikely to change its statutes to give Canada special status on subsidies and countervailing duties. But if Canada and the United States could agree on a list of prohibited practices, Congress might find such a list acceptable. A public recognition that existing practices would be covered by a grandfather clause or subject to future negotiation might also be acceptable. Furthermore, if a process of consultation and mediation could be established to cover new practices, good progress could be made on one of the key trade issues.

On safeguards — emergency protection against import surges — I agree with Smith that both countries will need to retain safeguard provisions for political reasons. It would be desirable if both countries used such provisions only when the domestic injury is caused by trade barriers being lowered as part of any comprehensive trade agreement, but I doubt that Congress would find such an arrangement acceptable. Congress severed the link between safeguards and import barrier reduction in the 1962 trade bill. Furthermore, following recent presidential decisions not to impose relief under the escape clause, particularly in footwear in 1985, Congress now threatens to remove presidential discretion, except under exceptional circumstances. However, if exceptions are written into a 1987 bill, there is at least a possibility that trade with Canada could be an exception under some circumstances. Such an arrangement would reduce the likelihood that a precedent would be set for the upcoming multilateral talks.

Four things not dealt with in detail in Smith's paper deserve greater attention. First, although Smith mentions at the outset that one of the reasons Canada is seeking secure access is because of "the continual threat of unilateral changes in the rules of the game," he does not pursue this point. I believe that even the modest changes in U.S. law that I review above are going to be difficult to obtain for several reasons, not the least of which is that the authors of much of that trade legislation are still on Capitol Hill. But it may be possible for Canada to get special status in laws not yet written. If the trend in U.S. trade laws continues, as seems likely, Canada could benefit from getting exemption or special treatment under future trade remedy laws.

Second, trade law has become a growth industry in Washington, and enterprising lawyers have found ingenious ways to file complaints under the various trade statutes. When administrative interpretations change, laws are revised, and when election pressures loom on the horizon, lawyers shop around for different avenues to pursue their cases. This "forum shopping" suggests that the laws cannot be taken as separate, distinct entities. Instead, they are interrelated from a public policy point of view. If the negotiators tinker with one or more of the statutes, sufficient thought needs to be given as to how that will affect the caseload under other statutes.

Third, Smith only touches on the judicial review of trade cases, which has been expanding in the United States, but I regard this a very important factor in the interpretation of U.S. trade laws. As if two branches of the U.S. government were not difficult enough to coordinate on trade policy, now the courts are playing a larger role. Harassment or delay from the judicial process could become an even more significant issue in the future.

Fourth, I would put more emphasis than does Smith on the need for institution building to create an interface mechanism, to use John Jackson's term. In those areas where new substantive laws cannot be agreed on, procedural mechanisms could be developed to provide for consultation, mediation, and reconciliation of frictions and differences. Certainly, some mechanisms will be added to manage the economic relationship as circumstances change. A procedure for updating norms and rules over time will be essential.

Before concluding, let me raise one more potential problem for ultimately selling the results of any agreement to the respective domestic constituencies. All of this discussion has been about rule changes. There is little scope for reciprocity on rule changes; it is certainly difficult to assess quantitatively the impact of rule changes. In order for Congress to go along with changes in U.S. trade remedy statutes, the U.S. private sector will have to be vocal in its support of any reciprocal rule changes to which Canada agrees. Smith cites one possible reciprocal rule change concerning investment rules, where Canada's unilateral changes have been a source of friction in the past. Changes in rules on services — including investment banking — and on intellectual property — particularly compulsory licensing — are two other possibilities. Without there being clear gains for U.S. domestic firms, I am concerned that private-sector lobbying on Capitol Hill will be insufficient to sell the package.

On a positive note, there is nothing like a deadline to force action. The negotiators have established September 1987 as their target deadline in order to submit a package to Congress under the fast-track process. I doubt, however, that a substantive agreement could be reached by then. But if the negotiators should miraculously achieve an agreement before the end of September 1987, then another problem probably will arise. Two trade bills would be moving through Congress at the same time, one implementing the bilateral trade agreement and the other extending authority. These bills then might be on a collision course; they almost certainly would be related to one another. The administration would have to work closely with key members of the Senate Finance and House Ways and Means Committees to avoid a congressional derailment of the agreement.

If the agreement slips past the fall of 1987, I believe the ultimate deadline will come in early 1988. It is my judgment that the negotiations must be completed during the remainder of President Reagan's term, if they are going to be completed at all. To push beyond 1988 would get the bilateral negotiations hopelessly enmeshed in the ongoing multilateral talks. Also by late 1988 or 1989, the Mulroney government will have to face the Canadian electorate. If there is little to show for the bold effort to negotiate with the United States, the negotiations could become a political football in Canada, as they have been so often in the past. In short, if 1988 passes without an agreement, the probability of failure will increase dramatically.

The pressures of time limits, top-level political intervention, the spotlight of public commitment, and the fear of failure are needed to close agreements. And despite what I have said about the lack of preparation, the United States comes close to developing a coherent trade policy only when it is forced to by the dynamics of international negotiations. So there is still hope. But precious time is slipping by. The clock is ticking and the groundwork, both analytically and in terms of domestic consensus building, is lagging. Unless there is sufficient direction from above and a firm delegation of responsibility to complete an agreement, it may well turn out to be an impossible task.

What would be the consequences of failure? First, it would not be a good demonstration effect to the rest of the world if the two most like-minded countries fail to agree. It could undermine the multilateral talks. The bilateral talks are like a mini-multilateral — most of the issues are the same. Whatever the United States and Canada obtain bilaterally on many of these issues is probably the most that can be hoped for in dealing with the rest of the world.

Second, U.S. trade strategy would be undermined. The threat of the United States' concluding bilateral agreements with like-minded countries has been one of the best weapons to pull some reluctant countries to the multilateral bargaining table. Such countries do not want to see Canada and the United States enjoy trade privileges in each other's markets that are denied to the rest of the world. Some countries also fear that a proliferation of bilateral deals would undermine the multilateral system. But if the multilateral process should collapse, successful bilateral negotiations with Canada would enhance the chances of concluding similar bilateral pacts with other like-minded countries. Failure of these bilateral negotiations probably would preclude that possibility.

Third, U.S. and Canadian firms would lose an opportunity to expand into a major industrial market. Firms on both sides of the border surely would face greater uncertainty in dealing with the other country. Export-oriented jobs would be jeopardized and the opportunity to rationalize North American production by achieving economies of large scale would be squandered.

Lastly, trade frictions — and other foreign policy frictions — between the two countries would increase in the wake of failed negotiations. If the option of concluding a special agreement with the United States is removed, Canada likely would turn inward and be less supportive of U.S. security and defense initiatives. A key U.S. ally — and one that houses a good portion of the U.S. defense umbrella — would be alienated.

Let me conclude by urging the private sectors in both countries to mobilize and submit their lists of grievances and to work with their respective governments to move these negotiations forward. In the United States, the administration must put more of an effort into these negotiations. It needs to be more ambitious and to raise its sights higher. It needs to prepare the analytic work and mobilize staff throughout the agencies. It needs to pay higher attention to the negotiations in order to develop a strategy that will lead to an agreement that is in the best interests of the American people. In Canada, the analytic work has proceeded quite far, but much more consensus building needs to be done to bring along the provinces. With some prodding from the private sector, perhaps both governments will get their acts together to complete these historic negotiations. The policy initiative is sound, but its execution is lacking. Let's get going! The window of opportunity is closing.

Comments

Gary N. Horlick

Murray Smith correctly points out that what we are really talking about is the investment climate. Investments made today are going to be producing goods and services in the 1990s. In the highly interdependent economies of our two countries, trade laws have an important influence on business decisions.

The fundamental purpose of trade negotiations and trade law rules is to create a stable environment for investment decisions. That is the purpose of the General Agreement on Tariffs and Trade (GATT), and it would also be the purpose of a bilateral U.S.-Canadian trade agreement. GATT rules may seem to be about current imports or exports but, starting with binding of tariffs, their real object is to allow businessmen to plan for the future. Although GATT rules on trade are much maligned, they are not that bad. The problem is that no one lives up to them and no one complains about it formally.

The symmetry of the U.S. and Canadian trade rules is worth noting. The two countries' antidumping rules are pretty much the same, with some odd quirks that would provide fodder for analysts of national character. The Canadian perception is that Canada is much burdened by U.S. trade cases. Yet, GATT statistics for the 1980–84 period show that U.S. authorities investigated seven antidumping cases and eight countervailing duty cases against Canadian products. By contrast, Canada had 20 antidumping cases (but no countervailing duty cases) against the United States during the same period.

This leads to several thoughts. One would assume that the United States has no subsidies — a notion which any U.S. taxpayer will cheerfully disclaim. Indeed, it is worth emphasizing that there is now a Canadian countervailing duty case against U.S. corn exports — the first such case ever brought against the United States. This is a tremendously significant step because, until now, Congress has acted as if the United States was invulnerable. One of the reasons why countervailing duty cases are the United States' chosen weapon is that no one ever used that weapon against the United States. Indeed, part of the problem is that no one countervailed the Domestic Insurance Sales Corporation (DISC) when the United States had that particular tax incentive, even though it was a fairly crude export subsidy. When the United States countervailed regional subsidies to Michelin Tire in Nova Scotia, it was really an investment dispute — a bidding war between Nova Scotia and Akron, Ohio. It was not a question of one side offering fair subsidies and the other side unfair subsidies. I do not believe Michelin really cared whether or not the offers were fair, just who was offering more.

There is a clear perception within the U.S. government (both Congress and the administration) that the United States is pure and the rest of the world is unfair. It makes foreign companies dealing in the United States absolutely livid. In the past year, while defending countervailing duty cases, I have had occasion to go through the published annual reports of three very large Canadian companies looking for soft loans from Canadian governments that U.S. industries complain about. One's eyes run down column after column until finding a U.S.$50 million loan at 8 percent interest. That sounds like a below-market rate, and it was, but it was for a subsidiary in the *United States* — industrial development bonds given to the Canadian company's U.S. subsidiary in Massachusetts or Alabama to build a factory. One can infer from this that Canada should start more countervailing cases against the United States, in order to raise the consciousness of Congress. If cheap timber is a subsidy to softwood lumber in Canada, then the U.S. timber tax capital gains system is even more a subsidy to U.S. softwood lumber and paper products going to Canada. Logically, then, one could have a Canadian case against U.S. paper products or lumber or other products.

Is this a good thing? No. Lawyers in Washington, and now in Toronto and Ottawa, could replicate the effects of the protectionist 1930 Smoot-Hawley tariff using a countervailing duty statute. One might find, for example, that police protection is more valuable to a bank than to a farmer. In the complete absence of publicly funded police protection, a bank presumably would have to pay more for insurance or private security measures than would a farmer. One can take this approach of countervailing any conceivable subsidy to absurd extremes. Is that a good thing? No. I would take it as a fairly good rule of thumb that more trade is better than less trade. More companies will be profitable and people will live better, and so on. So I would suggest that both countries are heading down the wrong path for their own economic good, and part of the reason is that the United States has this distorted perception of its own purity regarding subsidies.

That said, what could be negotiated in trade law rules between the United States and Canada? As several observers have pointed out, an exemption from U.S. trade laws is unlikely for political reasons. Beyond that, one would not want a complete exemption but, rather, something more like what Smith refers to as "national treatment". There probably should be rules against some unfair practices.

First, there should be rules of some kind against predatory pricing. The problem is that neither country's current antidumping laws have even a vague connection to sound economic theories of predatory pricing. Instead, they are a chess game for market share. In an ideal world, both governments could get rid of market-distorting antidumping laws and replace them with a much more economically based concept of predation, one that allows competition to proceed on a market basis. Both countries' overall economies would be better off, and companies on both sides of the border would still be protected in some way against anticompetitive practices.

Second, there should be rules against subsidies. Most businessmen I know do not like their competitors getting subsidies. They do not want to have to compete with other countries' or cities' or states' treasuries. What is more interesting is that businessmen do not always like receiving subsidies, either. Many have told me that they have to accept subsidies because their competitors are getting them. Subsidies not only help lead to budget deficits and exchange-rate problems but also distort what business is supposed to be about. Ideally, a bilateral agreement would include some system for getting rid of distortive subsidies, probably through a joint tribunal. As Smith notes, the European Community (EC) has such a system (rather than a countervail law), and there are about 100 cases a year in the EC where one company or country will complain about what another company or country is getting or providing in the way of subsidies.

Turning from idealism to reality, neither country is likely to get rid of antidumping laws, given the current political climate. This is unfortunate because such laws are costly to the economy. They have become enormously complicated, and they chew up reams of paper, lots of computer time, and lots of lawyers' time, all of which is a good thing from my point of view, but a bad thing from the point of view of business or the average citizen. It is going to be very difficult to negotiate anything on subsidies and countervail because the United States has this perception that Canada is unfair, while it refuses to acknowledge its own subsidization. As Smith points out, this is the worst possible time to be negotiating on these issues, given the large U.S. trade deficit. A much better time would be when things are brighter for both countries or when the United States is running a trade surplus rather than a deficit. Of course, if the United States was running a trade surplus, would Canada still be interested in negotiating a trade deal?

A further point on the practical side is whether a dispute resolution mechanism could be negotiated. The question that always arises here is: Would such a mechanism be binding or nonbinding? I do not mean that in any technical legal sense, but simply: Would the decisions count or not? If the decisions counted, the mechanism would be *very* useful. As I have said, there are actually pretty decent rules in the GATT. The problem has been their administration in both Canada and the United States. If a binding bilateral tribunal existed to which industries on both sides of the border could take complaints, then a fair and impartial decision would take care of a lot of problems. The trouble with such tribunals is that they require countries to give up what is referred to fondly as "sovereignty". Whenever it is a question of sovereignty, governments on both sides start sending up red flags and opposition parties start screaming no matter what side of the fence they are on. Label it as something other than sovereignty, however, and such a plan might be acceptable. Indeed, all countries have had to give up a lot of sovereignty to live together.

The other extreme is a "merely" advisory body, and when I say "merely" advisory I am suggesting that it is not worth much. Suppose, for example, that whenever a U.S. countervailing duty case was filed, the case went ahead but a study group was set up at the same time. In an extreme case, it might take a year for the group to report back. By then, the case might be long since over and no one would pay attention to the study.

There is probably a middle ground, with a nonbinding study group that would give both governments something to hide behind. Suppose the issue of subsidization of fish is raised. Although I am biased on this issue, as I defended the Canadian fishing industry, it is obvious that both sides are subsidized. The question is, How large are these subsidies? A nonbinding study might make a neutral assessment saying "this side gets this amount of subsidies and that side gets that amount, here is the state of the resource, and here is the answer." Both governments then could hide behind it and use it as an excuse to cut the subsidies they want to cut anyhow. U.S. government agencies would love an excuse to improve fisheries management in New England but they do not have any leverage, so they could use such a study as a lever. A tribunal does not have to be binding to have an effect; it really depends on how much the two governments want to use it.

Short of a total exemption, and in addition to a nonbinding tribunal, there is a long list of very technical things that could be negotiated to reduce the potential for harassment under both countries' laws. Let us take one example. Both countries have independent tribunals to decide questions of injury. The procedure is to send a questionnaire to everyone in an industry asking how much profit they have made over the past three years. If the companies are making higher and higher profits, it is hard to say they are being injured by imports. Not impossible, but difficult. There have been a number of cases, at least in the United States and, I suspect, in Canada, where injury has been found even though less than 15 percent of the companies in the industry bothered reporting their profits. It is difficult to think that an industry as a whole was severely injured by imports if 85 percent of that industry did not even bother answering the question. That kind of result simply leads to irritation on the other side of the border. A technical agreement on the evidence of, and standards for, injury determination would make the trade laws serve their stated purpose.

Other points that could be negotiated — some of which Smith discusses in his paper — include the following:

• *A commonly agreed list of prohibited domestic subsidies.* Such a list might have eliminated the shifting sands surrounding the concept of "specificity" that led to two countervailing duty investigations against Canadian softwood lumber products in three years, with totally different results so far.

The concept of specificity is basic to the countervailability of a domestic subsidy. The U.S. Department of Commerce and Revenue Canada countervail only those domestic subsidies that are specific to an industry or a group of industries. All governments undertake policies that affect economic production. These policies range from the very general (such as educating the labor force), to the very specific (such as providing direct grants to keep a faltering firm in production). There is no easy economic rationale for deciding which economic policies are too general to justify a countervailing duty, and which are specific enough to warrant such duties.

Although it is clear that such broad economic policies as police protection do not fall within the scope of the countervailable domestic subsidy definition, uncertainty exists with respect to policies such as Canadian provincial timber stumpage programs, unemployment insurance, regional development programs, U.S. agricultural programs, local development initiatives, and research and development funding. A commonly agreed list of prohibited domestic subsidies could help clear the air and provide a more predictable investment environment on both sides of the border.

• *More rigorous "standing" requirements.* Such requirements could have spared Canada from the recent countervailing duty cases on

swine and pork, and fresh Atlantic groundfish. Standing requirements limit a party's right to commence an antidumping or countervailing duty proceeding. Simply stated, a petitioner must produce
a "like product" in order to commence a proceeding. Recently, the
United States has relaxed its standing requirements and has permitted unqualified parties to commence a multitude of antidumping and countervailing duty proceedings. By agreeing to more
rigorous standing requirements, the two countries could limit greatly the harassment potential of their respective antidumping and
countervailing duty laws.
• *Revision of the de minimis definition* (the level of subsidy that
triggers a complaint). Such a revision could eliminate duties being
imposed on Canadian industries where dumping and subsidies are
found to be inconsequential. The U.S. Department of Commerce's
present *de minimis* threshold is 0.5 percent. If the two countries
could agree to a *de minimis* definition of perhaps 3 percent, their
respective antidumping and countervailing duty laws would be better able to provide the relief for which they were originally designed.
• *A commonly agreed standard of disclosure of information —
"transparency".* At present, neither country's antidumping and
countervailing duty laws provide full disclosure of information to
the parties of a proceeding. A common standard of disclosure would
permit confidential information to be scrutinized (by counsel sworn
to confidentiality) and tested, thereby improving the quality of the
information on which decisions are based, lessening the likelihood
of costly appeals, and increasing public confidence in the entire
process.
• *Negotiated limitations on the concept of "cumulation"* . In their
injury determinations, the Canadian Import Tribunal and the U.S.
International Trade Commission (ITC) cumulatively assess the
volume and effects of imports from two or more countries of like
products subject to investigation if such imports compete with each
other and with like products of the domestic industry. This practice recently resulted in an adverse finding against Canada's fresh-
cut flower industry, which, although its annual U.S. exports are less
than U.S.$250,000, was "lumped in" with eight other countries
whose total annual exports are well over U.S.$10 million. Had the
Canadian industry been considered separately, the ITC likely would
have found that Canada's minimal market penetration had not
caused injury to the U.S. industry.

If Canada and the United States are able to agree on a common
trade dispute resolution mechanism, they will also have to agree on

a common set of rules and definitions. Agreement on the matters outlined above would constitute a good starting point.

The key obstacle to negotiation of these issues is finding the political will. Political will is unlikely, however, unless the business communities of both countries push for it. The negotiators have had a series of sessions to explore the issues, but neither side has given any hints as to what it wants. This is one of the problems; negotiators on both sides need to be perceived at home as tough. They have to have politicians saying "our tough trade negotiators wouldn't give a thing." Of course, if neither side gives a thing, nothing happens and no deals are struck.

A final point worth mentioning is that Capitol Hill has provided no encouragement at all to the U.S. side to do anything about U.S. trade laws. Quite the contrary. If you accept that the issue of U.S. trade laws is of central importance to Canada in the negotiations, then so far the United States has turned a deaf ear to what Canada wants most. Negotiating anything on trade laws right now, or at least anything substantial, is going to be extremely difficult because there is no push within the United States from the private sector to obtain a more open and predictable bilateral trade regime. It is necessary to put the trade laws issue in a broader context. What is needed is an agreement that would permit businessmen in both countries to plan their investments on the basis of open and stable trade and investment rules.

Members of the Canadian-American Committee

at the time of the September 1986 meeting of the Committee

LAWRENCE BURKHART
President, Canadian Kenworth
Company, Mississauga, Ontario

DAVID J. BUTTERS
Senior Vice President, Shearson
Lehman Brothers Inc., New York, N.Y.

ROBERT W. CAMPBELL
Chairman and Chief Executive Officer,
Canadian Pacific Enterprises Ltd.,
Calgary, Alberta

TOM CAMPBELL
Chairman, Ontario Hydro,
Toronto, Ontario

JOE E. CHENOWETH
Executive Vice-President,
International, Honeywell Inc.
Minneapolis, Minnesota

PETER A. CHERNIAVSKY
President, BC Sugar, Vancouver, B.C.

WILLIAM COATES
Executive Vice President,
International, Westinghouse Electric
Corp., Pittsburgh, Pennsylvania

W.A. COCHRANE
Chairman and Chief Executive Officer,
Connaught Laboratories Limited,
Willowdale, Ontario

MARSHALL A. COHEN
President & Chief Operating Officer,
Olympia & York Enterprises Limited,
Toronto, Ontario

BASIL COLE
Counsel, Hamel & Park,
Washington, D.C.

THOMAS J. CONNORS
Executive Vice President, Operations,
Pfizer International Inc.,
New York, N.Y.

JAMES A. CURTIS
President and Chief Executive Officer,
Milliman and Robertson Inc.,
Seattle, Washington

A.J. deGRANDPRE
Chairman, Bell Canada Enterprises
Inc., Montreal, Quebec

WILLIAM DIEBOLD
Upper Nyack, N.Y.

THOMAS W. diZEREGA
Upperville, Virginia

WENDY DOBSON
President, C.D. Howe Institute,
Toronto, Ontario

RODNEY S.C. DONALD
Chairman, McLean, Budden Limited,
Toronto, Ontario

CHARLES F. DORAN
Professor and Director, Center of
Canadian Studies, Johns Hopkins
University, Washington, D.C.

JAMES L. DUNLAP
President and Chief Executive Officer,
Texaco Canada Inc., Don Mills, Ontario

MARCEL DUTIL
Chairman and Chief Executive Officer,
Le Groupe CANAM MANAC,
Ville St-Georges, Beauce, Quebec

WILLIAM A. ENOUEN
Vice President-Pulp Affiliates,
Mead Corporation, Dayton, Ohio

DONALD K. FARRAR
Senior Executive Vice President,
Textron, Inc., Providence, R.I.

JOHN FISHER
President, Southam Inc.,
Toronto, Ontario

THOMAS F. FLEMING
President, Morgan Bank of Canada,
Toronto, Ontario

JOHN R. FORREST
Senior Vice-President, Boise Cascade,
Boise, Idaho

FRED FOSMIRE
Senior Vice President, Human
Resources-Technology-Engineering,
Weyerhaeuser Company,
Tacoma, Washington

PETER GORDON
Managing Director, Salomon Brothers
New York, N.Y.

JAMES K. GRAY
Executive Vice-President, Canadian
Hunter Exploration Ltd.,
Calgary, Alberta

WILLIAM HAMILTON
Executive Secretary, Canadian
Federation of Agriculture,
Ottawa, Ontario

JOHN A. HANNAH
President Emeritus, Michigan State
University, East Lansing, Michigan

WILLIAM B. HARRISON
Executive Vice President,
Chemical Bank,
New York, N.Y.

WILLIAM R. HARRIS
Senior Vice-President, International,
PPG Industries, Inc.,
Pittsburgh, Pennsylvania

DONALD L. HART
Vice President-Bearings North and
South America, The Timken Company,
Canton, Ohio

JOHN B. HASELTINE
Senior Vice-President, First National
Bank of Chicago, Chicago, Illinois

ARDEN R. HAYNES
Chairman, President and Chief
Executive Officer, Imperial Oil
Limited, Toronto, Ontario

J. PAUL HELLSTROM
Managing Director, The First Boston
Corporation, New York, N.Y.

LAWRENCE C. HOFF
President, The Upjohn Company,
Kalamazoo, Michigan

BRUCE HOWE
Chairman and Chief Executive Officer,
Westar Industries, Vancouver, B.C.

E. SYDNEY JACKSON
Chairman and Chief Executive Officer,
The Manufacturers Life Insurance
Company, Toronto, Ontario

DAVID L. JOHNSTON
Principal and Vice-Chancellor, McGill
University, Montreal, Quebec

VERNON T. JONES
President, The Williams Companies,
Tulsa, Oklahoma

JOHN F. KEYDEL
Executive Director, Touche Ross
International, New York, N.Y.

JAMES KILTS
President & General Manager, Kraft
Limited, Montreal, Quebec

MICHAEL M. KOERNER
President, Canada Overseas
Investments Limited,
Toronto, Ontario

B.K. KOKEN
President and Chief Executive Officer,
Abitibi-Price Inc., Toronto, Ontario

Hon. MARC LALONDE
Stikeman, Elliott, Advocates,
Montreal, Quebec

LANSING LAMONT
Director, Canadian Affairs, Americas
Society, New York, N.Y.

SPERRY LEA
Vice President, National Planning
Association, Washington, D.C.

J. MAURICE LeCLAIR
Chairman and Chief Executive Officer,
Canadian National Railway Co.,
Montreal, Quebec

PHILIP B. LIND
Senior Vice-President, Rogers
Cablesystems Inc., Toronto, Ontario

FRANKLIN A. LINDSAY
Chairman, Vectron, Inc.,
Cambridge, Massachusetts

PIERRE LORTIE
President and Chief Executive Officer,
Provigo Inc., Montreal, Quebec

Hon. DONALD S. MACDONALD
McCarthy & McCarthy,
Toronto, Ontario

H. IAN MACDONALD
President Emeritus & Director, York
International, York University
North York, Ontario

ROBERT M. MacINTOSH
President, The Canadian Bankers'
Association, Toronto, Ontario

JOHN MACNAMARA
Chairman and Chief Executive Officer,
The Algoma Steel Corporation
Limited, Sault Ste. Marie, Ontario

RAYMOND MAJERUS
Secretary-Treasurer, United Auto
Workers, Detroit, Michigan

PAUL M. MARSHALL
President and Chief Executive Officer,
Westmin Resources Limited,
Calgary, Alberta

EDWARD E. MASTERS
President, National Planning
Association, Washington, D.C.

JAMES G. MATKIN
President and Chief Executive Officer,
Business Council of British Columbia,
Vancouver, B.C.

A.V. MAURO
President and Chief Executive Officer,
The Investors Group,
Winnipeg, Manitoba

JAMES A. McCAMBLY
President, Canadian Federation of
Labour, Ottawa, Ontario

W. DARCY McKEOUGH
McKeough Sons Company Limited,
Chatham, Ontario

JAMES A. MERRILL
Senior Vice President and Chief
International Economist,
Marine Midland Bank, N.A.,
New York, N.Y.

JOHN MILLER
Vice Chairman, National Planning
Association, Washington, D.C.

FRANK J. MORGAN
President & Chief Operating Officer,
The Quaker Oats Company,
Chicago, Illinois

FRANK E. MOSIER
President, The Standard Oil Company,
Cleveland, Ohio

J.J. MUNRO
President, Western Canadian Regional
Council No. 1, International
Woodworkers of America,
Vancouver, B.C.

RICHARD W. MUZZY
Vice Chairman of the Board,
Owens-Corning Fiberglas Corporation,
Toledo, Ohio

OWEN J. NEWLIN
Senior Vice President, Pioneer Hi-Bred
International, Des Moines, Iowa

ROBERT G. NICHOLS
Partner, Price Waterhouse,
New York, N.Y.

JAMES NININGER
President, The Conference Board of
Canada, Ottawa, Ontario

GORDON OSBALDESTON
Senior Fellow, School of Business
Administration, University of
Western Ontario, London, Ontario

RICHARD B. PATTON
Senior Vice President, H.J. Heinz
Company, Pittsburgh, Pennsylvania

CHARLES A. PERLIK, Jr.
President, The Newspaper Guild
(AFL-CIO, CLC), Washington, D.C.

CHARLES PERRAULT
President, Perconsult Ltd.,
Montreal, Quebec

ROBERT L. PIERCE
President, NOVA, An Alberta
Corporation, Calgary, Alberta

JOHN W. PITTS
President, MacDonald, Dettwiler &
Associates Ltd., Richmond, B.C.

GEORGE J. POULIN
General Vice-President, International
Association of Machinists and
Aerospace Workers, Washington, D.C.

WILLIAM S. RANDALL
President, Chief Executive Officer,
and Chairman of the Board, First
Interstate Bank of Washington, N.A.,
Seattle, Washington

ROBERT REISER
Group Vice President and President,
International Operations,
Xerox Corporation,
Stamford, Connecticut

DAVIS R. ROBINSON
Pillsbury, Madison & Sutro,
Washington, D.C.

RAYMOND ROYER
President and Chief Operating Officer,
Bombardier Inc.,
Montreal, Quebec

A.E. SAFARIAN
Department of Economics, University
of Toronto, Toronto, Ontario

JAMES R. SCHLESINGER
Senior Advisor, Shearson Lehman
Brothers, New York, N.Y. and Senior
Advisor, Center for Strategic
International Studies, Georgetown
University, Washington, D.C.

J. MICHAEL G. SCOTT
Vice-Chairman, McLeod Young Weir
Limited, Toronto, Ontario

JACK SHEINKMAN
Secretary-Treasurer, Amalgamated
Clothing and Textile Workers' Union
(AFL-CIO, CLC), New York, N.Y.

CHARLES SITTER
Director and Senior Vice President,
Exxon Corporation,
New York, N.Y.

RAY V. SMITH
President and Chief Executive Officer,
MacMillan Bloedel Limited,
Vancouver, B.C.

RICHARD STOVER
Senior Vice President, Global
Marketing Group, Mellon Bank,
Pittsburgh, Pennsylvania

JOHN SWEENEY
President, Service Employees
International Union (AFL-CIO, CLC),
Washington, D.C.

JAMES C. TAYLOR
President, Morgan Stanley Canada
Limited, Toronto, Ontario

KENNETH D. TAYLOR
Senior Vice-President, Government
Affairs, Nabisco Brands, Inc.,
New York, N.Y.

W. BRUCE THOMAS
Vice Chairman — Administration and
Chief Financial Officer, USX
Corporation, Pittsburgh, Pennsylvania

ALEXANDER C. TOMLINSON
Executive Director, Center for
Privatization, Washington, D.C.

PETER M. TOWE
Chairman, Petro-Canada International
Assistance Corporation, Ottawa, Ontario

GEORGE E. WARDEBERG
Vice Chairman and Chief Operating
Officer, Whirlpool Corporation,
Benton Harbor, Michigan

R.D. WENDEBORN
Executive Vice President,
Ingersoll-Rand Company,
Woodcliffe Lake, N.J.

P.N.T. WIDDRINGTON
President and Chief Executive Officer,
John Labatt Limited, London, Ontario

WILLIAM P. WILDER
Chairman, The Consumers' Gas
Company Ltd., Toronto, Ontario

LYNN R. WILLIAMS
International President, United
Steelworkers of America
(AFL-CIO, CLC),
Pittsburgh, Pennsylvania

L.R. WILSON
President and Chief Executive Officer,
Redpath Industries Limited,
Toronto, Ontario

FRANCIS G. WINSPEAR
Edmonton, Alberta

GEORGE W. WOODS
Vice-Chairman, TransCanada
PipeLines Limited, Toronto, Ontario

CHARLES WOOTTON
Coordinator, International Public
Affairs, Chevron Corporation,
San Francisco, California

Honorary Members

M.W. MacKENZIE
Ottawa, Ontario

JOHN R. WHITE,
New York, N.Y.

Sponsoring Organizations

The C.D. Howe Institute is an independent, nonpartisan, non-profit research and educational institution. It carries out, and makes public, independent analyses and critiques of economic policy issues and translates scholarly research into choices for action by governments and the private sector.

The Institute was created in 1973 by a merger of the C.D. Howe Memorial Foundation and the Private Planning Association of Canada. The Foundation had been created in 1961 to memorialize the late Right Honourable C.D. Howe, who served Canada in many elected capacities between 1935 and 1957, including as Minister of Trade and Commerce. The Private Planning Association of Canada was a unique forum created in 1958 by leaders of business and labor for the purpose of carrying out research and educational activities on economic policy issues.

While its focus is national and international, the Institute recognizes that Canada is composed of regions, each of which may have a particular perspective on policy issues and different concepts of what should be national priorities.

A Board of Directors is responsible for the Institute's general direction and for safeguarding its independence. The President is the chief executive and is responsible for formulating and carrying out policy, directing research, and selecting staff. In order to promote the flexibility and relevance of its work, the Institute's high-quality professional staff is intentionally kept small and is supplemented by a program of visiting professionals and links with a number of scholars and compatible institutions.

Participation in the Institute's activities is encouraged from business, organized labor, trade associations, and the professions. Through objective examinations of different points of view, the Institute seeks to increase public understanding of policy issues and to contribute to the public decisionmaking process.

Grant L. Reuber is Chairman, Wendy Dobson is President and Treasurer, and Brenda Huff is Corporate Secretary.

The Institute's offices are located at: Suite 900, 555, boul. Dorchester ouest, Montréal, Québec H2Z 1B1; P.O. Box 1621, Calgary, Alberta T2P 2L7; and 125 Adelaide Street East, Toronto, Ontario M5C 1L7.

The National Planning Association (NPA) is an independent, private, nonprofit, nonpolitical organization that carries on research and policy formulation in the public interest. NPA was founded during the Great Depression of the 1930s when conflicts among the major economic groups — business, labor, agriculture — threatened to paralyze national decisionmaking on the critical issues confronting American society. It was dedicated to the task of getting these diverse groups to work together to narrow areas of controversy and broaden areas of agreement and to provide on specific problems concrete programs for action planned in the best traditions of a functioning democracy. Such democratic planning, NPA believes, involves the development of effective governmental and private policies and programs not only by official agencies but also through the independent initiative and cooperation of the main private-sector groups concerned. And to preserve and strengthen American political and economic democracy, the necessary government actions have to be consistent with, and stimulate the support of, a dynamic private sector.

NPA brings together influential and knowledgeable leaders from business, labor, agriculture, and the applied and academic professions to serve on policy committees. These committees identify emerging problems confronting the nation at home and abroad and seek to develop and agree upon policies and programs for coping with them. The research and writing for these committees are provided by NPA's professional staff and, as required, by outside experts.

In addition, NPA's professional staff undertakes research designed to provide data and ideas for policymakers and planners in government and the private sector. These activities include the preparation on a regular basis of economic and demographic projections for the national economy, regions, states, metropolitan areas, and counties; research on national goals and priorities, productivity and economic growth, welfare and dependency problems, employment and manpower needs, energy and environmental questions, and other economic and social problems confronting American society; and analyses and forecasts of changing international realities and their implications for U.S. policies.

NPA publications, including those of the Canadian-American Committee, can be obtained from the Association's offices, 1616 P Street, N.W., Suite 400, Washington, D.C. 20036.